Dynamic
Literacy Instruction:

Using a Dispositions Approach
for Professional Development

Dynamic
Literacy Instruction:
Using a Dispositions Approach
for Professional Development

by

Susan E. Israel, PhD

Independent Literacy Consultant

Christopher-Gordon Publishers, Inc.
Norwood, Massachusetts

Copyright Acknowledgments

Christopher~Gordon Publishers, Inc.
Bridging Theory and Practice

1420 Providence Highway, Suite 120
Norwood, MA 02062

800-934-8322 • 781-762-5577
www.Christopher-Gordon.com

Printed in the United State of America
10 9 8 7 6 5 4 3 2 1   10 09 08

ISBN: 978-1-933760-11-7
Library of Congress Catalogue Number: 2007929379

Contents

"Nothing is predestined: The obstacles of the past can become gateways that lead to new beginnings."

—Ralph Blum

Dedication

I would like to dedicate this book to
my loving husband, Kevin,
who has inspired me to set goals
and achieve them as well.

Preface

"It takes great goals to lead us out of our everyday limits into accomplishing more than we ever thought we could or would."

—Robert Cooper

Powerful Goals for Exemplary Literacy Teachers: An Interactive Teaching Tool through Self-Reflection and Collaboration was written to help all teachers who influence literacy learning and who want to understand why teaching behaviors, regardless of grade level or content area, play a key role in achievement and motivation. As one reviewer stated so eloquently,

---

Parker Palmer's *Courage to Teach* speaks about the 'inner landscapes of teachers' that we bring to our teaching. He writes, 'I project the condition of my soul onto my students, my subject and our way of being together.' He goes on to say, 'When I do not know myself, I cannot know who my students are. I will see them through a glass darkly, in the shadows of my unexamined life ~ and when I cannot see them clearly, I cannot teach them well.

This book is written in an easy-to-read format that may be used as an interactive teaching tool to engage the reader in self-reflection of behaviors that are characteristic in exemplary literacy teachers. As the reader, you will participate in self-reflection through assessment of current teaching behaviors, engage in reflective thinking based on my personal reflections and teaching stories that permit the activation of familiar teaching experiences, and with guidance from the text, use the information with self-reflection to change behaviors in order to achieve the instructional literacy goals of this book.

This book happened naturally out of my ten years of teaching experiences in the elementary classroom, and from teaching undergraduate and graduate level literacy courses, which results in about twenty plus years of teaching. The dispositions or behaviors of exemplary teachers of literacy are the focus of the goals described in this book and the awareness of how teaching behaviors influence instruction, as well as student motivation, achievement, and decisions about personal and professional goals.

Teachers Thinking Differently About Being an Exemplary Literacy Teacher

According to Harris and Hodges (1995), there are five definitions that describe the word literacy. There are no definitions that describe a literacy teacher. To me, a literacy teacher is one who develops student's reading, writing, speaking, listening, and thinking. In reality, all teachers are teachers of literacy, regardless of their title or specialization.

A powerful learning experience in my undergraduate children's literature course, which eventually became the "inner" seed that germinated the idea for this book, had to do with the concept of "values." As an assistant professor, I was teaching the course for the first time. My goal was to meet the needs of my students while effectively teaching content about children's literature. One way to determine if I am being an effective teacher is to obtain data about my teaching through student evaluations. Prior to this course, my teaching evaluations as a new professor seemed to be all over the board. This means in student terms, "She is the best professor I have ever had" or "She is the worst professor I have ever had."

Subsequent to one of my classes around mid-semester, I was having a discussion with my husband about how I could improve my teacher evaluation scores. My husband asked one simple question, "What is it that your students value in your class?" He then stated, "You need to find out what it is they value and focus on those values in relationship to the course objectives. This will take care of your teacher evaluations." That was the end of our conversation.

His reply, as brief as it was, made sense. I needed to find out what it was that my students' valued and determine how best to use those values to guide instruction in the course while meeting the needs of my students. At the time the conversation with my husband occurred, I was finishing my book on metacognitive literacy instruction *Metacognition in Literacy Learning,* so I knew that reflection was an important tool that could help me find out what it was my students valued.

The next day, I started class with a children's read-aloud called *ish* by Peter Reynolds (2006): a story about thinking differently on how we see the world. After that, I asked my students to take out a sheet of scrap paper and respond to the question, "What is it that you value most in this class and why?" I collected the papers and put them in my briefcase so that I could read them that evening. I thanked my students for taking the time to respond to my question told them I was going to use their responses to guide the course goals for the remainder of the semester.

Reading students' responses about my teaching have always been a difficult experience for me. For me, it is difficult to hear negative comments about things I take seriously and put so much effort into. Sometimes when I am reading my teacher evaluations at the end of the semester, I wonder if they are actually my teaching evaluations. I always think, "This can't possibly be true about me." For example, I have read, "This teacher is so unprepared for class and she is disorganized." To read responses like this makes me furious because I spend so much time preparing for my courses and organizing my materials for class. I have always taken pride in being organized. So reading or thinking about my weaknesses that others point out to me, which may or may not be true, is still difficult.

I knew that reading my responses about what my students valued would be difficult because I had no idea what to expect. The first response I read said the following, "What I value most in this class is that you value me." The "why" read, "you demonstrate that you care about us, you are positive, you ask us what is important in our lives, and you take time to teach us about research that we can use." I was so awe-struck by what this student wrote. I had no idea that this would be something that students would value. I honestly thought they would write about the literacy books I share with them because they want to learn about good teaching resources, or about how effective my PowerPoints are because they can transfer this knowledge to their own teaching experiences in order to change or guide instruction.

It took several days for me to read the rest of the responses. I did not want to address any negative responses from students nor did I want to feel lousy about myself as a teacher, but I knew that in order for me to become a better teacher, I needed to change. A professor once told me when I was going through my post-graduate courses to obtain my PhD that the positive responses never seem to matter. One negative response is all you focus on and that response will outweigh all the positive ones, but try to use the negative responses as measures for improvement. The secret is to take the negative responses and to turn them into ways to measure areas for improvement. Eventually, I read all the students' responses and discovered several behaviors I needed to change. I share them with you to help you realize that self-reflection and assessment is not an easy process. I would share with you all my positive comments, but that would simply be an act of vanity. Below are a few of their comments, which give some indication as to what and how I needed to change. The first part is what the student wrote that he or she valued. The italics represent what I inferred as specific areas to address within this course and with my instruction.

- I value more discussions about current events in literacy. *Add more discussion time about current events in literacy based on student interests.*

- I do not value all the handouts because there are too many. *Instead of making handouts, place them online for students to obtain as needed. Write on the handouts the purpose for each handout and the benefits to the teacher, as well as my rationale for providing the handout in the first place.*

- I need more information about reading levels of books and how to use leveled books in the classroom. *Research leveled books and how students can use this knowledge when making book selections in their classroom. Encourage them to read books about leveling. During read aloud in class, use different leveled books on the same topic and give ideas on how to use them in content areas.*

- Give more websites we can use in our teaching. *Instead of making more handouts, place websites on the board and a brief annotation about why this website is valuable. Add links to my teacher homepage that will benefit students when teaching.*

- I would appreciate more time in class to work on sharing our teaching ideas from the author studies and from the literature binders. I value time to learn more from my peers. *Allow more time in class to discuss projects. Encourage students to dialogue about how their ideas have made a difference in their beliefs about teaching or pedagogy.*

Examining Literacy Behaviors through Goal-Setting Strategies

When I invited students to share their values about teaching, I was motivated to investigate research in the area of teaching behaviors, and dispositions associated with exemplary literacy teachers, and the standards driving the dispositions and research. Thinking differently about exemplary literacy teaching and behaviors became the inspiration to write this book. The decision to use the format of self-reflection and goal setting as a method to evaluate pedagogical beliefs, and teaching behaviors to improve literacy instruction is based on my own experiences, my knowledge of metacognition, and my desire to strive to be exemplary. As teachers, if we do not strive to be exemplary, we will not be able to effectively address the achievement issues we face today. If you believe the most important person who can be the agent of change in the classroom is the teacher, this book is for you. If you do not believe this, perhaps reading this book will help you see that a teacher's disposition can influence literacy achievement outcomes.

This book will guide you through inner reflection about what lies beneath the teaching knowledge and skills exposing good teaching behaviors that should be exemplified by literacy teachers. Most likely, you chose to be an educator because you desire as I do to help all children become lifelong literacy learners. This book is meant as a tool for professional development and growth, in the intellectual sense, as well as in the emotional sense. In this book, you will discover how to reflect upon and attain six behavior-oriented teaching goals that make a difference in helping children become lifelong literacy learners. The six goals outlined in this book are:

- Enthusiasm
- Unity
- Kindness
- Understanding
- Pursuit of Knowledge
- Collegiality

The goals are supported by national and international professional organizations' dispositions and teaching guidelines, research on the characteristics of exemplary literacy teachers, and personal teaching experiences related to literacy and the integration of literacy in content areas. It is through this support that I hope you become empowered to reflect deeply on your teaching behaviors. As the reviewers of this manuscript have so eloquently pointed out, there can be many ways to define and interpret the concept of "dispositions." This book is being written to help literacy teachers' awareness of how behaviors can effect teaching instruction in the classroom. I offer my interpretation of the dispositions that are being used at the time of publication of this book as a starting point for teacher reflection and discussion, not a definitive response. I am not going to argue that there are only six behaviors that teachers should set as goals to achieve. My own personal search on the Internet gives insight into the many different interpretations of educational institutions and associations. I argue that as teachers, we should pay attention to one's behavior regardless of whether if it is called enthusiasm, gusto, passion, zeal, or any other synonym that describes a teacher's disposition about literacy. The point really is that teachers should demonstrate this enthusiasm. As a reader you might be encouraged to challenge the different labels I have used to define the dispositions, but I ask that your time be spent in using this book as the tool that it is meant for and that is to guide self-reflection on the very act of teaching and all the behaviors associated with it. If I were defining the dispositions during the early days of literacy pioneers, I might have used very different descriptors. I hope this book will be used as a tool to guide powerful goals that reflect behaviors of exemplary literacy teachers, not as a weapon to debate ways to describe dispositions.

The format of this book is in a style to provide the reader with an interactive reading experience and is suitable for individual, small-group, or school professional development materials. The rationale for the dispositions are introduced and explained in relationship to literacy instruction. Each goal has been given a descriptive word that summarizes the corresponding disposition making or behavior to achieve, which will provide the reader easy way to make associations with teaching behaviors in order to understand and apply in the literacy classroom.

Schunk (200) defines a goal as something that reflects one's purpose and performance. He explains goal setting as the process of establishing a standard or objective to serve as the aim of one's actions (p. 100). Based on goal theory readers set a purpose for reading and work toward achieving that goal by evaluating their progress along the way. Goal setting is also a great motivational and metacognitive tool that teachers can apply in their own classrooms. This book will make a successful contribution to the field of literacy and teacher education if literacy teachers use the thoughts generated through personal reflections to evaluate, integrate, and enhance literacy learning for all students. The goals will guide the reader into thinking more deeply about teaching behaviors or dispositions that influence literacy. The goals guide the behaviors; it is up to the reader to guide change.

- To achieve the goal of enthusiasm you will learn how to value reading and writing and model this behavior in the classroom
- To achieve the goal of unity in your classroom you will learn how to create opportunities for all students, especially those most at-risk or from diverse populations
- To achieve the goal of kindness you will maintain a classroom that is built on positive literacy engagements and environments
- To achieve the goal of understanding you will develop an attitude that views assessment as essential to understanding students' strengths and areas for improvement
- To achieve the goal of knowledge you will develop a passion for professional development opportunities to enhance literacy pedagogy
- To achieve the goal of collegiality you will learn how to foster positive collaborations with colleagues and those in the larger school community in order to advance literacy learning, motivation, and professional growth

In summary, this book will take you on an inner teaching journey using self-reflection as the motivation for change. The easy-to-follow self-guiding approach will scaffold you, a study group, or professional development session toward reflection that promotes change. Before reading the next section, take a few minutes to reflect on your prior teaching experiences in relationship to your teaching behaviors. Use the space below to write down your thoughts as you reflect on the following questions.

 How would you describe your teaching behaviors that influence *student learning* in your classroom or teaching experience?

_____

_____

_____

_____

_____

_____

_____

How would you describe your teaching behaviors that influence *student motivation* for literacy learning?

_____

_____

_____

_____

_____

_____

_____

How would you describe your behaviors that influence your *professionalism* and *professional development*?

_____

_____

_____

_____

_____

_____

_____

How would you describe the behaviors of *exemplary literacy teachers?*

_____

_____
_____
_____
_____

_____

_____
_____
_____

Acknowledgments

I would like to express my sincerest thanks to Christopher-Gordon Publishers who afforded me the opportunity to work with such an efficient editorial staff. I would also like to thank Troy Donovan for his help with the production of this book.

It is with deepest gratitude that I wish to thank Sarah M. Luckhaupt and E. Camille Yancey, former students from the University of Dayton for sharing their wisdom and knowledge about the future of teaching. Thank you for being such wonderful and supportive education majors.

Introduction

Reflecting on Behaviors of Exemplary Literacy Teachers

"Not everything that can be counted counts, and not everything that counts can be counted."

—Albert Einstein

Powerful Goals for Exemplary Literacy Teachers is an interactive teaching tool for self-reflection and increased professional growth for educators at all levels who desire to examine their teaching behaviors and pedagogy. Educators, such as classroom teachers, and content area teachers who work directly with children will benefit from reading this book. Administrators or district planners can use this book as a manual to facilitate professional development either during in-service programs or with small study groups within the school community. The theoretical foundation for using goals and self-reflection as a tool for teacher examination and change is supported by metacognition (Flavell, 1979; Israel et al., 2005). Based on the tenets of metacognitive theory, the format of this book is written in a reflective and interactive style, which allows you to think about your thoughts related to teaching behavior and literacy instruction. If you respond "yes" to any of the questions below, you will benefit from reading this book.

- Are you interested in reflecting on the dispositions of your literacy teaching?
- Do you need help in learning how to self-direct professional growth?
- Are you in a situation that might be too restrictive for your creative and technical abilities and need a teaching resource that offers hope?
- Do you want to improve teaching behaviors so that your instructional delivery is received effectively?
- Are you an educator who is committed to your work but need a recourse that will allow you to take a peaceful retreat geared to your own needs?
- Are you an administrator or district leader, who works with many teachers and needs a tool to support professional growth?
- Are you planning an in-service with specific goals that will allow educators to examine instruction through self-discovery, as well as grow professionally through collaboration?

Regardless of your reason for reading this book, the benefits will vary by the degree to which you allow yourself to be open to personal and professional change. With that being said, there are many ways to engage in reading this book in order to maximize the learning experience.

As a Tool to Fuel Professional Growth

If you are interested in fueling your professional growth and inquiry in all aspects of teaching, you might decide to read the chapters sequentially. While reading you can follow along with prompts that invite you to deeper reflection on certain aspects of teaching related to the goal you are trying to achieve. You may also decide to read this book selectively. In that case, you can begin by overviewing the table of contents and select chapters highlighting specific goals that you want to develop.

As a Tool to Guide Inquiry Group Discussions on Exemplary Literacy Behaviors

This book can be used as a tool to guide a group through strategies that will impact change in behaviors in order to improve literacy instruction. The questions and self-reflection prompts can be used to stimulate conversation about important problems and possible solutions that teachers face in today's busy classrooms. You could enjoy discussing the book during a series of lunch study groups or after school. Inquiry groups who are doing teacher research on exemplary literacy instruction can use this book to evaluate the affective domains of teaching.

As a Facilitator's Guide During In-service/Professional Development Workshops

If your school district is in the process of evaluating characteristics that contribute to student achievement and motivation, this book can be read to build background knowledge in the area of effective research-based literacy practices. This book addresses key issues that school districts face. Issues that school districts are facing that are addressed in this book include: how to engage diverse learners, how to integrate and use assessment instruments effectively, how to motivate increased levels of reading in the classroom and home environment, how to develop positive rapport with students and parents, and how to value professional development opportunities to effectively impact literacy instruction.

As a Scaffold for Literacy Coaches and Reading Specialists

If you are a literacy coach or reading specialist, you will find the self-reflections with the literacy goals to help you when conducting in-school professional development days. The questions for reflections can be used to guide discussions. The problems and solutions can be used to facilitate discussions on similar problems. The research presented with the literacy goals, as well as the standards matrix in Section I will also provide you with the evidence to support exemplary literacy behaviors all teachers should exhibit in the classroom and larger school community.

Explanation of Powerful Goals

The chapters that follow this introduction will offer an in-depth guided investigation for each of the six goals highlighted below. As explained in the preface, the references to each of the six goals represent my best interpretation of teaching dispositions as outlined from primary sources of national and international teaching and literacy organizations, as well as related research and my experiences. In response to a comment to a reviewer of this manuscript who was concerned about the techniques chosen and the foregrounding on why to use dispositions at all: The rationale for selected techniques is based on my best response to current issues and relevant and available research on each topic that would benefit literacy educators. The techniques are not a prescription for success, but are offered as starting points for investigation and self-reflection. A unique feature in this book is the recommendations for further resources on key ideas in the chapter, which also make available further topics for discussion and personal growth. Likewise, the foregrounding for the dispositions will be up to the reader to decide based on individual situations, professional expertise, and various levels of teaching, as well as systematic school-wide goals, just to mention a few. My foregrounding for the dispositions are based on the need to summarize key behaviors of exemplary literacy teachers so that future teachers and teachers in need of renewal and professional growth will benefit. Before reading this book, you might want to think about what dispositions you hold as most important? What dispositions or behaviors are included in your school's mission or vision statement? I offer the following dispositions to set as goals for exemplary literacy instruction:

- *Enthusiasm: Teacher Demonstrates a Love of Reading and Writing.* This goal focuses on beliefs and attitudes of effective teachers of reading regardless of their content area. Reading becomes the link to aid the teacher in meeting each unique student's desire for learning based on the personal interests of the student and his or her individual style of learning. I begin with the goal of enthusiasm because the love of literacy must start with the teacher.

- *Unity: Teacher Creates Opportunities for Diverse Learners.* This goal will aid the teacher in meeting diverse learners' academic needs as well as social needs. Teachers will understand how the concept of unity is important when trying to build community and meet the needs of individual learners. The goal of unity follows enthusiasm because I believe building community in the classroom helps define students desire to learn. If students do not feel a sense of unity within the literacy community, their value and self-worth might become a factor for achievement. Teachers of at-risk students have enough factors or issues to be concerned about.

- *Kindness: Teacher Maintains a Positive Literacy Environment.* This goal will help teachers with organizing literacy classrooms regardless of content area or domain to encourage and promote positive classroom practices. Problems and solutions are relevant in today's classrooms where students desire to learn in a caring and supportive environment. Following unity is the goal of kindness. Certainly this can be placed anywhere in this book. I have placed it after unity because maintaining a positive literacy environment influences student motivation. Kindness is imbedded within the decision-making of the classroom, instructional delivery, and curricular choices.

- *Understanding: Teacher Recognizes Assessment as Essential to Discovery of Self and Students.* This goal will help teachers understand how assessment is used to guide instruction. Teachers learn how to overcome challenges through effective actions that promote an understanding of metacognitive assessments and administration of them to further discovery of self and students. The goal of understanding follows because it is important that instructional goals be guided by assessment and student feedback; therefore, holding the disposition of understanding in order to recognize discovery of self and students is important. The reader should keep in mind that the dispositions are not linear but interwoven.

- *Pursuit of Knowledge: Teacher is Passionate about Professional Development.* This goal will help teachers evaluate their behaviors related to personal and professional growth. Teachers will discover how research and service improves literacy instruction and student learning. The goal of pursuit of knowledge is placed before collegiality because the disposition of pursuit of knowledge through professional development must happen first from within before others factor into the development of dispositions characteristic of pursuit of knowledge.

- *Collegiality: Teacher Fosters Positive Collaborations in the School and Community.* This goal will aid teachers in forming positive and valuable collaborations with peers, parents, and the larger school community. Lastly, I explain how collegiality fosters positive collaborations with others. Others in the school are those adults who we work with within our school, or study group setting. Collegiality, although placed last in the book, is carried equal weight with the previous five dispositions.

Features that Foster Self-Reflection and Professional Growth

At the beginning of each chapter are self-assessment questions that guide teacher thinking and reflection on the chapter's goal. Throughout the chapter, prompts will help you evaluate your progress and document your teaching observations, reactions to literacy goals when applied in the classroom and literacy successes that have fostered change within the affective domain of teaching with the goal of increasing student learning, motivation, and personal professional development. Suggestions on what the literacy goal will look like in exemplary literacy classrooms when planning for literacy instruction will be provided. In addition, you will set future goals to help you maintain exemplary literacy behaviors you have achieved from engaging in the professional development experience presented in this book.

The book offers many unique features to guide teachers through a self-awareness of effective teaching behaviors, which are realized through setting and achieving goals. Each goal follows a consistent pathway to goal attainment using a metacognitive process. Each chapter begins with teaching reflections about exemplary literacy teachers. The teaching reflections are included to help you recall unforgettable teachers who made a positive impact on your literacy development. What attributes made these teachers exemplary? What can you learn from these teachers to help you achieve exemplary literacy behaviors?

Figure 1.1 provides a visual to help understand the organizational features in each chapter.

- "Self-reflection on Theory and Practice" will introduce the reader to aspects of the disposition by engaging the reader through motivational stories, quotes or poems, uses self-assessment questions that help reflect on prior knowledge, outlines chapter goals, and provides supporting research.

- "Self-questioning to Evaluate Behaviors" will help the reader formulate a plan and continues to build on the foundation of the literacy goal. This section will provide the reader with an opportunity to think critically about the teaching practices related to the goal through problems teachers might encounter that keep them from achieving the literacy goal and research based solutions to help them toward achieving the goal.

- "Self-monitoring to Achieve Goal" will provide the reader the opportunity to bring together the foundational knowledge and self-discovery of the goal's theme and guide the reader by establishing strategies that will connect the research to practice. A goal-monitoring checklist will help the reader self-monitor the literacy goal and provide literacy teachers with effective strategies to overcome today's toughest literacy issues. The chapter will close with a final section called, "Thinking Deeply." This section concludes with three elements. Strategies to help those who want to reflect more deeply or engage in discussions with peers. Enrich personal or professional understanding of the literacy goal by reading additional references recommended by the author. Finally, for those who like to engage in writing as a form of reflection, the chapter concludes with space for journal reflections.

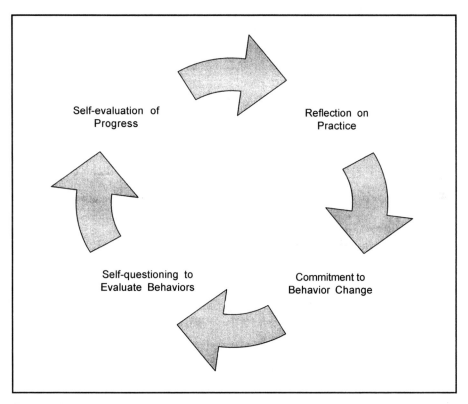

Figure 1.1   Illustrates the literacy goal process that is used in each chapter to outline interactive procedures to achieve literacy goal in each chapter.

This book offers a deeper understanding of how teaching behaviors influence all aspects of effective literacy instruction. The main goals for this book are as follows:

- Develop an awareness of how literacy behaviors influence student learning, motivation, and professional growth by focusing on characteristics that reflect inner qualities of exemplary teachers.
- Examine teaching behaviors through metacognitive reflection.
- Increase knowledge of how literacy dispositions integrate with knowledge and skills of teaching.

- Create opportunities for increased literacy teaching and self-efficacy related to literacy instruction through self-reflection and professional development.
- Understand how to integrate the six powerful literacy goals in a literacy classroom in order to enhance student learning and motivation

Reflection is an important part of self-discovery and improved teaching of literacy instruction. This book provides the foundation for literacy teachers to reflect on their teaching behaviors and set personal goals to improve literacy instruction.

Support for Literacy Teaching Dispositions

Merriam-Webster's Collegiate Dictionary 11th Edition defines a disposition as the dominant quality or qualities distinguishing a person's mood or attitude about life around them. The International Reading Association defines dispositions as:

> The values, commitments, and professional ethics that influence behaviors toward students, families, colleagues, and communities and affect student learning, motivation, and development as well as the educator's own professional growth. Dispositions are guided by beliefs and attitudes related to values such as caring, fairness, honesty, responsibility, and social justice."
> (Standards for Reading Professionals, 2003, p. 29)

Related synonyms to describe dispositions are:

- temperament
- temper
- moral fiber
- character
- spirit
- personality

A common saying using the word is, "He or she has such a pleasant disposition." How would you finish the sentence, "I have a _____ disposition about literacy teaching?" Are you passionate? Do you show compassion? Are you wise? Do you strive for justice?

Looking inside yourself and reflecting on your inner teaching spirit will enable you to transform your dispositions to reflect those of exemplary literacy teachers. Parker Palmer believed in the teacher's inner spirit. What I found interesting in his book *A Hidden Wholeness* was the way he described personal transformation.

> First, we all have an inner teacher whose guidance is more reliable than anything we can get from a doctrine, ideology, collective belief system, institution, or leader. Second, we all need other people to invite, amplify, and help us discern the inner teacher's voice. (Palmer, 2004, pp. 25–26)

Allow the teacher's inner spirit in you and this book to discern your inner teacher's voice. Literacy goals summarized in this book are guided by professional and literacy organizations' standards on dispositions.

Professional Standards of Dispositions

Each goal is supported by the dispositions and guidelines set by the International Reading Association, National Council for Accreditation of Teacher of Education, and Interstate New Teacher Assessment and Support Consortium.

International Reading Association (IRA) Synthesis of Dispositions

The Standards for Reading Professionals (2003) provide criteria for assessment of performance for reading professionals. Reading professionals include paraprofessional, classroom teachers, reading specialists, literacy coaches, teacher educators, and administrators. Dispositions of reading professionals are described in Standard 5 on Professional Development. Table 1.1 summarizes the elements of professional development disposition.

The International Reading Association is an advocate of professional development. The dispositions outlined in Table 1.1 support the six literacy goals summarized in each chapter.

Table 1.1   Elements of IRA's Professional Development Dispositions

Disposition Description	What This Looks Like For Reading Professionals
Displays positive dispositions related to reading and the teaching of reading (5.1)	• Respects students • Models ethical and caring attitude of reading • Articulates theory and research connections • Ensures ethical literacy context
Pursues development of professional knowledge (5.2)	• Studies aspects of reading • Demonstrates curiosity • Identifies inquiry questions • Pursues answers to inquiry • Informs about literacy issues • Supports literacy advocates • Conducts and participates in study groups • Reads professional journals • Conducts research • Supports colleagues
Works with colleagues to provide feedback on practice (5.3)	• Engages in collaboration • Communicates evidence • Conducts action research • Evaluates own and other's teaching • Reflects to improve practice • Encourages dialogue
Participate in and initiate professional development programs (5.4)	• Participates individually or with colleagues • Exhibits leadership skills in professional development • Prepares and coach colleagues • Participates in professional development at the national level • Provides opportunities for professional development

National Council for Accreditation of Teacher of Education (NCATE) Synthesis of Dispositions

Professional standards for the accreditation of schools, colleges, and departments of education are guided by the knowledge, skills, and dispositions of the National Council for Accreditation of Teacher Education. NCATE establishes teaching standards that are assessed based on performance. According to NCATE Standards, "Dispositions are not usually assessed directly. Instead dispositions are assessed along with other performances in candidates' work with students, families, and communities" (NCATE Standards, 2002, p. 19). Because dispositions are assessed with other performances related to knowledge and skills, it is difficult to determine what behaviors influence student learning, motivation, and professionalism.

NCATE's visions that 21st-century teachers are "caring, competent, and highly qualified teachers who teach every child." Significant aspects of the standards are the conceptual framework, which is the underlying structure that sets forth a vision and provides direction for theoretical and philosophical paths. The dispositions, as explained above, are woven into the threads of the conceptual framework. A recent survey conducted by NCATE (Drew & Tande, 2006) examined how dispositions are implemented in teaching. The results indicate a need to define dispositions and outline effective behaviors. The survey also suggests that a process on how to develop dispositions needs to be clarified. A majority of the respondents in the survey agreed or strongly agreed that dispositions can be changed. Typically, in the past, teacher dispositions are reported as being assessed prior to teacher education programs or during student teaching. The reports of the survey address the need for a resource that defines dispositions, provides a mechanism for self-discover to promote change, and communicates effective teaching practices influenced by one's disposition during their career. This book responds to this need.

The NCATE standards define target dispositions indirectly. Standard 1: Candidates' Knowledge, Skills, and Dispositions emphasize that candidates work with students, families, and community in ways that reflect the disposition expected of each professional educator. The dispositions are based on standards of the Interstate New Teacher Assessment and Support Consortium (INTASC), which are derived from the Council of Chief State School Officer (CCSSO). Information can be found at www.ccsso.org/intasc.html. In addition, when thinking about dispositions, NCATE recommends thinking about codes of ethics, specifically the codes of ethics as outlined by National Education Association and International Reading Association. Information about NEA can be found at www.nea.org. Table 1.2 outlines the elements of teaching dispositions as defined by INTASC.

Table 1.2   Elements of INTASC's Professional Development Dispositions

INTASC Standard	Summary of description of dispositions
Standard 1: Subject Matter	• Teacher realizes subject matter as complex and seeks to learn new ideas in field. (1.21) • Teacher appreciates multiple perspectives and conveys to learners how knowledge is developed. (1.22) • Teacher has enthusiasm for content. (1.23) • Teacher is committed to continuous learning. (1.24)
Standard 2: Student Learning	• Teacher appreciates individual variations and shows respect for diverse talents. (2.21) • Teacher uses students' strengths as opportunity for learning (2.22)
Standard 3: Diverse Learners	• Teacher believes all children can learn. (3.21) • Teacher values diversity. (3.22) • Teacher respects students as individuals with differing personalities and backgrounds. (3.23) • Teacher is sensitive to community. (3.24) • Teacher makes students feel valued. (3.25)
Standard 4: Instructional Strategies	• Teacher values development of students' performance. (4.21) • Teacher values flexibility as necessary for adapting instruction to student learning. (4.22) • Teacher values educational technology to promote learning. (4.23)
Standard 5: Learning Environment	• Teacher establishes positive climate. (5.21) • Teacher understands how participation supports commitment. (5.22) • Teacher values role of students in promoting learning and values peer relationships. (5.23) • Teacher recognizes value of intrinsic motivation to learning. (5.24) • Teacher is committed to each child's development and uses a variety of motivational strategies to develop learning. (5.25)

(Continued on next page)

Table 1.2   Elements of INTASC's Professional Development Dispositions *(Continued)*

INTASC Standard	Summary of description of dispositions
Standard 6: Communication	• Teacher recognizes the power of language for learning. (6.21) • Teacher values different ways to communicate. (6.22) • Teacher is a thoughtful and responsive listener. (6.23) • Teacher appreciates cultural dimensions of communication. (6.24)
Standard 7: Planning Instruction	• Teacher values long and short-term planning. (7.21) • Teacher believes plans might change based on needs of students and community. (7.22) • Teacher values planning as a collegial activity. (7.23)
Standard 8: Assessment	• Teacher values ongoing assessment. (8.21) • Teacher is committed to using assessments to identify student strengths for learning opportunities. (8.22)
Standard 9: Reflection and Professional Development	• Teacher values self-directed learning. (9.21) • Teacher is committed to reflection, assessment, and learning as an ongoing process. (9.22) • Teacher is willing to give and receive help. (9.23) • Teacher seeks out opportunities to refine practice that addresses individual needs of students. (9.24)
Standard 10: Collaboration, Ethics, and Relationships	• Teacher values all aspects of a child's experience. (10.21) • Teacher is concerned about all aspects of child's well-being. (10.22) • Teacher respects privacy of students. (10.23) • Teacher is willing to consult with other adults about well-being of students. (10.24) • Teacher is willing to work with other professionals to improve learning environment. (10.25)

Note: For a complete description of each standard and description consult the Interstate New Teacher Assessment and Support Consortium.

Reflecting on Literacy Teaching Dispositions

Now you have an understanding of what the professional and literacy organizations define as dispositions. It is your turn to reflect on whether it is evident in your practice if you display the dispositions. Use the Teaching Dispositions Self-Assessment in Table 1.3 to help you understand your inner spirit of teaching from a dispositional perspective. Use this self-assessment to reflect on your practice and areas for improvement or invite your students to respond to the statements.

Table 1.3   Teaching Dispositions Self-assessment

Directions: Read the following belief statements and explain your beliefs about literacy teaching behaviors.

Goal to Achieve	Personal Statements and Responses
Enthusiasm for Literacy	I have enthusiasm for reading and writing and demonstrate this when I... I recognize the value of intrinsic motivation to learning and how my behaviors influence students intrinsic motivation when ...
Unity for all Learners	I value diversity and demonstrate this when I... I value peer relationships in the learning process and use peers as an opportunity to include others when I... I appreciate individual variations and shows respect for diverse talents when I...
Kindness Toward Students	I establish a positive climate by... I respect students as individuals when I... I make students feel valued everyday when I...

(Continued on next page)

Table 1.3   Teaching Dispositions Self-assessment *(Continued)*

Goal to Achieve	Personal Statements and Responses
Understanding Students Through Assessment	I value ongoing assessment by using the following assessments ... I value development of students' performance by communicating to them their... I value flexibility as necessary for adapting instruction to student learning when assessments illustrate student weaknesses and I ...
Knowledge of Content	I appreciate multiple perspectives and convey to learners how knowledge is developed when I... I value educational technology to promote learning and this is demonstrated when I... I realize subject matter as complex and seek to learn new ideas in field when I participate in...
Collegiality with Colleagues	I value planning as a collegial activity and demonstrate this daily when I... I value different ways to communicate to my peers when I struggle by... I am a thoughtful and responsive listener because I know when to...

Which dispositions are strongly evident in your practice? What do you feel to be the greatest strength and weakness of your teaching? How would your students rate you on each of the dispositions in Table 1.3? Consider using this assessment with your students to understand their perspective on your teaching behaviors and attitudes about student learning, motivation, and professionalism.

The literacy goals summarized in this book are to help you achieve exemplary literacy instruction in your classrooms. The literacy goals are supported by IRA, NCATE, and INTASC standards. For additional reflection on standards-based dispositions, use the standards outlined by your area of expertise or the ones based on your grade, such as the Standards published by the National Middle School Association.

Summary

In summary, you have been introduced to the six goals of exemplary literacy teachers and the supporting standards based on the dispositions associated with literacy professionals. You have also reflected on your own beliefs about your instructional and professional behaviors. Perhaps your unforgettable teacher is a teacher you had in grade school, or perhaps your unforgettable teacher is your current graduate level professor. You can use the space provided in this book for some of the reflection prompts or use your own journal for more space. Use the dispositions self-assessment to respond to the following questions or use your responses to guide discussion with your colleagues.

 What do you expect to gain from reading *Powerful Goals for Exemplary Literacy Teaching*?

_____

_____

_____

_____

_____

_____

_____

What misconceptions do you have about teaching dispositions?

_____

_____

_____

_____

_____

_____

_____

_____

Do you think dispositions are an important aspect that will influence your ability to change pedagogy?

_____

_____

_____

_____

_____

_____

_____

_____

If you are reading this book with a study group, what are the group goals to be achieved?

_____

_____

_____

_____

_____

_____

_____

_____

Are there other hidden dispositions that you think should be considered in order to deepen your practice? If so, what are they and how can they deepen your practice?

_____

_____

_____

_____

_____

_____

_____

What factors might keep you from behaviors that lead to exemplary literacy instruction?

_____

_____

_____

_____

_____

_____

_____

Goal #1: Enthusiasm

Teacher Demonstrates Passion for Reading and Writing

As a teacher, you have the responsibility to get your students excited and interested in literature. There are many ways that you can do this! One way is to surround your students with a print-rich environment...books, magazines, newspapers. Teachers should have books from all genres available and incorporate non-fiction into book studies, and whatever teachers are studying with your students. I believe every student has a love of reading if just surrounded by the right books.

—Katie, Pre-service teacher

Journaling Thoughts on Enthusiasm

This chapter focuses on helping teachers achieve the goal of being enthusiastic in the literacy classroom and learning how to overcome barriers that get in the way of demonstrating positive behaviors. This chapter also will help teachers at all levels understand that they are teachers of reading and writing and have a responsibility to use their enthusiasm to motivate individual student's quests for learning through meaningful literacy engagements.

Self-questioning to Achieve Goal

Why do you want to make a commitment to the learning behavior of Enthusiasm? Do you believe the goal will have an influence on instruction?

Thoughts for Group Discussion:

Rationale for Setting Goal of Enthusiasm

Based on teaching standards from literacy organizations, all teachers are expected to display positive dispositions related to reading and the teaching of reading in their classrooms.

Katie, a pre-service teacher believes it is the teacher's responsibility to get students excited about reading and writing. Do you believe it is the teacher's responsibility to be enthusiastic about reading and writing? Review your notes from Table 1.3, *Teaching Dispositions Self-assessment* from the disposition goal of Enthusiasm that you completed in the Introduction on pg. 14. Think about a time you were enthusiastic about reading and writing with your students. How did this experience make you feel? How do you think your enthusiasm increased student motivation? Use this reflection to help you evaluate your teaching behaviors related to your enthusiasm for reading and writing that you currently display with your students.

Self-Reflection: Making a Commitment

Findings from the Report of the National Reading Panel have changed the way literacy teachers think about teacher education and reading instruction with the goal of demonstrating the value of reading and writing was published by the National Reading Panel (NICHD, 2000). Findings from the report on teacher education and reading instruction are summarized in the following:

Teacher attitudes do change as a result of intervention in both pre-service and in-service contexts. This is an important finding because it is the predisposition of teachers to change that makes change possible. Without a change in attitude, it is extremely difficult to effect change in practice. (pp. 5–14).

According to Block, Oakar, and Hurt (2002) highly effective teachers display behaviors they most enjoy about literacy components. Exemplary teachers demonstrated high levels of enthusiasm, regardless of grade level, for literacy was used to establish a basis for motivation and positive rapport with students, which encouraged them to value literacy (Block, Oakar, & Hurt, 2002). The literacy goal of enthusiasm is worth pursuing to model for students the value of reading and writing to enhance individual quests for learning. What was interesting about this research on exemplary teachers was their desire to use instruction to motivate students. Exemplary teachers at each grade level valued reading and writing but demonstrated this value though actions appropriate for grade level students' needs. For example, enthusiastic characteristics to increase reading and writing in the primary grades were to use authentic explorations to ignite student interest levels. Second grade teachers demonstrated literacy as whole processes. By doing so, teachers were able to model how adults enjoy and value literacy so students also understand the importance. By the time students reached the upper grades, exemplary teachers in the study were highly sensitive to the amount of time they spent on concepts with increased levels of time spent on tasks based on what students believed was necessary to develop that concept. Time spent on boring instruction that was unnecessary was minimized due to the teacher's sensitivity to tasks that produce achievement results.

Additional research summarized in the 5th edition of the *Models and Processes of Reading* (Ruddell & Unrau, 2004) was updated to reflect the teaching of reading in the 21st century. In this publication, Allington and McGill-Franzen believe well-designed schools would have a rich supply of reading materials available for instructional use and more time available for teachers to be enthusiastic about literacy instruction.

Negative factors have the potential to restrict teachers from demonstrating enthusiasm for reading and writing tasks, which could factor into a teacher's ability or desire to change. The negative factors are summarized in Table 2.1 to help you reflect more deeply on how you display enthusiastic behaviors. The list of negative factors that have the potential to influence your ability to be enthusiastic about literacy in your classroom or situation were compiled from research (Allington & McGill-Franzen, 2004; Block, Oakar, & Hurt, 2002; Ruddell & Unrau, 2004). Reflecting on issues or attitudes that might consciously or subconsciously impact your attitude in the classroom will help you focus on your goals. Use the statements in Table 2.1 to prompt your thinking about actions that might contribute to a lack of enthusiasm for reading and writing. Check the statements that apply and record your reflections when you are finished in the space below.

Table 2.1   Factors that Minimize Enthusiasm Checklist

_____ 1. Teachers own negative attitude about reading and writing or belief that they are a poor reader or writer.

_____ 2. Crowded classrooms and not enough literacy resources to meet the individual and diverse needs of all learners.

_____ 3. Reading and writing materials that are not easy to implement or not appropriate for developmental levels.

_____ 4. Outdated literacy materials and a lack of funds to replace print-rich environmental resources.

(Continued on next page)

Table 2.1 Factors that Minimize Enthusiasm Checklist *(Continued)*

_____	5. Language barriers in books for English Language Learners and a lack of teacher knowledge or expertise on how to effectively help students.
_____	6. Lack of books that students are actually interested in and motivated to read.
_____	7. Time constraints due to mandated literacy curriculum and the lack of quantity and quality of reading and writing time.
_____	8. Parental constraints that keep you from time spent on planning rich literacy experiences.
_____	9. Issues related to environmental influences such as team teaching pedagogical differences.
_____	10. Affordable, high-quality literature or access to literacy resources when needed.
_____	11. Other Factors

Review the list and reflect on the negative factors you have checked. Do you notice any trends with your responses? Are there other factors that need to be considered?

_____

_____

_____

_____

_____

_____

_____

_____

_____

_____

_____

_____

_____

_____

_____

Observation from a Window into Literacy Lives

I attended the Scholastic Book Fair to purchase some new books that I could use in my classroom with my students and ones that I would also like to read. When I arrived, several of the older students were looking at the books and talking to each other. I was curious about what books they were interested in, so I asked them. One girl was very excited to tell me all about her new favorite books she wanted to purchase and read. Another girl waited to respond but continued looking at the books and was about to share with me her favorites when someone said, Dr. Israel, why do you want to know what books we like to read? I told the student that I thought it was important to read books that were exciting; not only to students but also that I would enjoy reading as well. The one girl who was looking over the books pointed to a book she wanted to read. The book was the sequel to one of my very favorite Newbery novels, Crispin, the Cross of Lead by Avi (2002). I was so excited that she pointed out the sequel to me and I could hardly wait to read it.

Consider going to a book fair or the library and ask students questions about what books they like to read. Have you shared your favorite books with students? How did they respond to some of your favorite books?

Self-questioning to Achieve Goal

What challenges do you experience that keep you from being enthusiastic about reading and writing?

How Colleagues Overcome Challenges:

What did you learn about your inner teaching self when considering a response to the statements above? What are enthusiastic behaviors related to reading and writing that you already possess that you could share with others? This section provides the reader with an opportunity to formulate a plan and respond to areas that will help improve your level of enthusiasm about reading and writing. Real-life problems related to reading and writing that might negatively influence a teacher's behavior are summarized below. Following the problems are ideas and strategies on how to approach the issues discussed and challenges teachers face. As you read the problems and solutions be-low and reflect on the information from your responses, consider the following questions:

- Do you see patterns emerging in your beliefs and specific problems generated by your emerging beliefs?

- How might your beliefs influence your teaching?

- What can you identify as a goal for yourself?

- How will you work toward this goal?

Challenges That Create Motivation for Change

Students who face reading difficulties constantly challenge literacy teachers at all grade levels. Student problems related to reading get in the way of maintaining a positive disposition. Teachers can benefit from this section by first reading the problem and reflecting on the explanations of the problem. In the following section is a research-based solution that will offer ideas on how to overcome the negative factors that might influence a teacher's disposition about promoting reading and individual quests for literacy learning.

When Teachers Who are Not Readers Realize They Are

One attitude that might hinder teachers from having a positive dispo-sition about the value of reading could be that the teacher is not a reader and does not enjoy reading. According to Powell-Brown (2004), it was difficult to understand how anyone could expect chil-dren to love reading and writing when the teacher was not a role model for reading and writing.

Teachers who do not enjoy reading can reflect on their own read-ing habits and develop strategies to change their personal beliefs about reading so as to promote a love of reading in their classroom. If you believe you are a non-reader, Powell-Brown (2004) provides some suggestions to develop the disposition of valuing reading to pro-mote students' individual quest for literacy learning. Chances are you might have always held the belief that you are not a reader or writer. Perhaps you had a negative experience during your formative years of teaching. Alternatively, perhaps you have not thought critically about the actual print-rich material but you enjoy reading that labels you as a reader.

Think about what you love about reading. If you do not like to read, think about why you do not like to read. What has contributed to you becoming a non-reader? If a particular teacher or person turned you away from reading, maybe you could try to confront that issue and develop a strategy on how to forgive that individual. You may say you are a non-reader but you go home at night and devour a newspaper. Does this still make you a non-reader? Teachers have an impact on why or why not students choose to read and what they might choose to read. What do you like to read? What print-rich material do you have in your home environment? If someone assessed me as being a reader or non-reader based on whether or not I enjoyed reading fiction, I would be labeled a non-reader. However, that assessment would not be very accurate because right now while I sit here writing this chapter I see the following in my home environment that clearly would label me as a reader.

- Biographies about famous world leaders such as Desmond Tutu
- *How to Quilt* books
- An entire collection of my favorite journal *Reading Research Quarterly* which came in the mail today
- Lots of picture books
- Poetry that my children have written for me
- Nature magazines such as *Smithsonian*
- Mickey Mouse Cookbook
- Newbery Books

If you consider yourself a non-reader, do some reflection on what it is you enjoy about reading and writing. Consider re-evaluating your position on whether you are a reader or writer based on your discoveries. If you still have trouble believing you are a reader, do the following:

- Make time to read and fake it until you make it
- Try to force yourself to find things that you enjoy reading
- If you cannot find anything to read, ask other colleagues who might have a similar negative attitude to make recommendations on what they like to read. Perhaps you might revisit old childhood favorites and rediscover the beauty of one of the characters in the book.
- Making time to read things that are of interest to you will improve your attitude about reading.
- Share reading experiences about books you enjoyed when you were younger. It doesn't matter what age or what level the book. Just give

students an opportunity to understand you as a reader and what books you did enjoy reading.

- Be a proponent for having frequent book discussions in your classroom. Share things that you are reading, such as newspaper articles or some interesting web sites where you learn about different topics that you can discuss in the classroom. Introduce students to print-rich materials such as your favorite magazines.

- Avoid asking students to do book reports on books they have read. Instead, have them create a project on what they experienced from reading a particular book.

- Invite guest speakers into your classroom who do love reading and ask them to share with your students their favorite books. Librarians are a wonderful resource and are very knowledgeable about favorite adolescent selections.

- Have reading mentors for all students. Give students opportunities to discuss their passions for reading or what happened to make them lose their passion.

- Change your way of thinking about reading time and create time where students are engaged in sustained reading and writing. Some students may not be readers, but a good teacher will recognize them and allow opportunities for writing instead of reading.

When Students Who Do Not Love Reading Learn How to Love Reading

Even though the teacher has a positive disposition about the value of reading, students might have negative attitudes about reading. It is the job of the teacher to promote reading, so factors associated with the development of a love of reading need to be investigated in order to promote individual quests for literacy learning.

Students who do not have a love of reading or can read but choose not to read can interfere with a teacher's disposition about the value of reading. Strommen and Mates (2004) surveyed a cross-section of middle school students in sixth and ninth grade attending a suburban middle school. The purpose of the research was to discover factors that contribute to and support a child's learning to love reading. Findings suggest that teachers can pay particular attention to several factors in order to help students develop a love of reading. One way to understand what your students perceive about your level of enthusiasm about reading and writing is to invite students to complete a Teacher's Enthusiasm for Reading and Writing Survey like the one in

Table 2.2. If you are a teacher of younger children who are not yet able to write, invite a teaching partner to assist you with administering the survey in small groups or use the primary inventory in Table 2.3.

Table 2.2   Teacher's Enthusiasm for Reading and Writing Survey

Directions: Respond to the following questions. Provide as much detail as you can when responding. You may have an adult help you record your answers if necessary.

1. How does your teacher demonstrate enthusiasm for reading and writing?

2. Give an example of when your teacher was enthusiastic about something you read or wrote. Why was this important to you?

3. Describe a situation the last time your teacher displayed enthusiasm about reading or writing?

4. Do you have any other suggestions on how you would like your teacher to be more enthusiastic with helping you learn about reading and writing?

5. Other Comments:

Table 2.3   Primary Teacher's Enthusiasm for Reading and Writing Inventory

Directions: Draw a face that represents how I display enthusiasm for reading and writing.

Survey Question	My teacher is not very enthusiastic	My teacher is sometimes enthusiastic	My teacher is very enthusiastic
Does my teacher demonstrate enthusiasm for reading and writing?			

(Continued on next page)

Table 2.3   Primary Teacher's Enthusiasm for Reading and Writing Inventory *(Continued)*

Survey Question	My teacher is not very enthusiastic	My teacher is sometimes enthusiastic	My teacher is very enthusiastic
Directions: Draw a face that represents how I display enthusiasm for reading and writing.			
My teacher is enthusiastic about something you read or wrote.			
My teacher demonstrates enthusiasm during read-aloud experiences?			
My teacher shares interesting books with us.			

Reading Engagements That are Meaningful

When engaged in literacy discussions about books or materials that the students are expected to read, classroom discussion is surface level and dominated by a few students. Furthermore, the topics being discussed do not seem to be relevant to the reading assignment or students' lives. Therefore, too few students are able to make meaningful connection with the material being discussed, causing frustrations for the teacher.

Many teachers use discussion as a tool to engage students in the content and to extend or elaborate on the material. If the teacher does not value helping students make meaningful connections, the discussion or conversation going on in the classroom would continue in the manner in which only a few students participate. Teachers who value promoting reading and individual quests for learning utilize strategies to solve this problem so that more students can actively participate in the discussion. Teachers might become frustrated when too few students are actively engaged, which contributes to unenthusiastic behaviors.

One strategy you can use is to reformulate your questions. Asking introductory questions to activate critical thinking would engage more students (Foster, 2004). Asking introductory questions to activate critical thinking will help adolescents and developmental levels consider how a problem or event can be related to life experiences. Foster increased discussion by using three different types of introductory questions: analogy, opinion, and imagination. An example of a lesson that integrates introductory questions to activate critical thinking is outlined below.

GOAL OF LESSON: To provide an opportunity for all students to be actively engaged in a discussion after reading the novel *To Kill a Mockingbird* by Harper Lee (1960) with the goal of increasing student motivation and enthusiasm for learning by valuing the amount of time spent engaging students in meaningful instruction.

METHOD FOR INSTRUCTION: Teacher explains the three different types of questions that students can respond to prior to beginning the class discussion. After the teacher explains the different types of questions, students can select one of the different introductory questions and respond in their journal.

Examples of Analogy Questions:

How are the two main characters alike?

What do books, magazines, and newspapers have in common?

Examples of Opinion Questions:

If you could design the perfect place for Miss Maudie to live, what would it look like?

How would you guarantee that Jem or Dill could learn in your classroom?

Examples of Imagination Questions:

If you were lost, what three things would you do to seek help and why?

If Mr. Finch won an award from the president, what type of award would that be and what three things would you do to celebrate this occasion?

DISCUSSION STRATEGIES: Teachers can elicit higher levels of critical thinking during discussion time by having students respond to the topic being discussed using one of the three types of introductory questions. Students can pair up with another child and have each student discuss their question. Once small groups have responded to the questions, teachers can begin a larger group discussion and invite students to share some of the questions and answers they thought demonstrated a critical analysis of the topic. Teachers can make sure that all students have an opportunity to participate in the larger classroom discussion, as well as provide evidence of why the responses are meaningful to them by sharing their personal stories or key discussion points.

DEVELOPING THE LITERACY GOAL: Taking time to monitor classroom discussions in a way that elicits richer and more meaningful conversations demonstrates that the teacher values time to promote reading while helping all children succeed in making meaningful connections. In addition, the integration of the literacy goal enhances the high standards you have already set in your classroom.

Three common issues that have the potential to keep teachers from being enthusiastic about reading and writing is their own perception about being a reader or writer, students who do not value reading and writing, and time spent on meaningless instructional engagements, which decrease teachers' interest levels and student motivation.

Take a few minutes to reflect and review the information you have gained thus far. If you are working with a study group, discuss the problems that negatively influence your ability to be enthusiastic about reading and writing and possible solutions.

 Challenges in my classroom that negatively influence my enthusiasm for reading and writing are:

_____

_____

_____

_____

_____

_____

_____

Strategies on how to overcome challenges and increase my enthusiasm for reading and writing are:

_____

_____

_____

_____

_____

_____

_____

_____

Self-evaluation of Progress

Self-evaluation of Progress

Have you achieved your goal? If not, what positive action can you take to achieve the goal?

New Ideas:

This chapter provided you with an opportunity to self-reflect and self-assess through questioning strategies, examples of negative factors that keep teachers from demonstrating enthusiasm, and examples of problems teachers might face in the classroom. Thus far, the following reading goals of this chapter have been realized:

- How reading and writing can be valued by the teacher so that all students can be successful
- What teachers can do to avoid negative behaviors for reading and writing

- How to model enthusiasm when facing difficult situations
- Strategies for how teachers can adjust reading behaviors to increase literacy connections for all students
- Use enthusiasm as a motivational strategy to engage students in meaningful learning experiences

The contents and organization of this chapter provided a scaffold to reflect on how reading and writing can be woven into our instructional practices so that all students can be successful in your classroom. Throughout the chapter, specific questions invited deeper reflection on critical aspects of reading behaviors that have the potential to prohibit students' literacy connections. Table 2.4 is a matrix of positive factors that increase enthusiasm for reading and writing. You can use this matrix for additional ideas to display the literacy goal of enthusiasm by focusing on how you can help yourself, your students, and the larger school community.

Table 2.4   Reflecting on Behaviors with the Goal of Increasing Enthusiasm

Understanding Factors That Reduce Enthusiasm	What Teachers Can Do For Inner Self	What Teachers Can Do For Students	What Teachers Can Do For The Larger School Community
Teacher's own negative attitude	Make a list of literacy things you feel positive about	Share your favorite childhood book and tell them why you liked it	Write a letter to communicate the things you have enjoyed doing related to literacy events
Crowded classrooms	Examine your schedule to see if you can work with smaller groups or teach in blocks	Minimize environmental clutter	Work with leaders to identify positive solutions to student classroom size
Reading and writing materials not appropriate	Visit the International Reading Associations website www.reading.org and print the Children's Choice Award Lists	Remove literacy resources and hold a school book sale to raise money for more appropriate materials	In your newsletter write about the exciting resources you wish you had and how they benefit students

(Continued on next page)

Table 2.4   Reflecting on Behaviors with the Goal of Increasing Enthusiasm *(Continued)*

Understanding Factors That Reduce Enthusiasm	What Teachers Can Do For Inner Self	What Teachers Can Do For Students	What Teachers Can Do For The Larger School Community
Lack of funds	Consider using more library or museum resources or contact book publishers like Harcourt Publishers Book Donation Team	Encourage students to participate in Scholastic, Trumpet, or Troll Book Orders Star teacher favorites	Swap classroom libraries with other teachers so new literacy materials are available
Language barriers	Learn more about the language or culture to minimize instructional issues	Invite students to share information about their culture and language	Host a cultural event sponsored by the students
Mandated literacy curriculum	Do more research on the curriculum to understand effectiveness	Do not complain about the curriculum in front of them	Do research on what highly effective whole school communities do to increase teacher enthusiasm about reading and writing
Environmental influences	Focus on more positive issues when in the presence of other teachers or school administration	Allow students to demonstrate their enthusiasm for reading and writing	Start a new program that you are enthusiastic about and let others get involved with it

Take a moment to identify a personal goal on how you can increase your level of enthusiasm for reading and writing in your teaching situation. If you are a classroom teacher, can you integrate a variety of read-alouds that are important to you? If you are a literacy coach, can you identify a belief that you have that increases your level of enthusiasm in order to help others? If you are an administrator, what can you do to create a more enthusiastic literacy environment in your school? If you are a professor, what problems do you think your students will face in today's busy classrooms that will keep them from being enthusiastic about literacy instruction and what solutions can you offer?

*My personal goal to help me be enthusiastic and demon-
strate a love of reading and writing to promote individual
quests for learning now is:*

_____

_____

_____

_____

_____

_____

_____

_____

_____

_____

The reason this goal is important to me is:

_____

_____

_____

_____

_____

_____

_____

_____

_____

_____

Prior to the conclusion of this chapter is a self-monitoring checklist
to help you evaluate your inner spirit for enthusiasm of reading and
writing.

Self-monitoring Checklist

Self-Monitoring Statement	Behaviors you Display	Actions to Take to Increase Enthusiasm
How do you value reading and writing in your classroom?		
Do you share some of their favorite books, as well as read excerpts from some of the books they are currently reading with your students?		
What other type of print-rich materials have you incorporated in your classroom?		
How have you promoted reading and writing in your classroom?		
Do you offer choices for students with special challenges?		
How have you adjusted your reading and writing instruction so that you are more enthusiastic? Have you permitted students to choose topics of interest?		
What positive actions can you take to help you monitor and achieve your personal goal?		

My Self-monitoring Checklist

Self-Monitoring Statement	Behaviors you Display	Actions to Take to Increase Enthusiasm
How do you value reading and writing in your classroom?	I like to start and end class with my favorite books and have students write in their journals everyday using prompts students have generated	I should try to share more books that students might be interested in rather than my own
Do you share some of their favorite books, as well as read excerpts from some of the books they are currently reading with your students?		I need to spend more time sharing some of the books students are reading in class and having them read some of their favorite excerpts
What other type of print-rich materials have you incorporated in your classroom?	I like to use magazines and plays	I like to have books on display in all areas of my classroom
How have you promoted reading and writing in your classroom?		
Do you offer choices for students with special challenges?	I try to incorporate a lower level reading book	I need to work on using more technology with special needs students who might struggle with reading so as not to undermine their abilities
How have you adjusted your reading and writing instruction so that you are more enthusiastic? Have you permitted students to choose topics of interest?	I try to avoid negative comments about how disappointed I am about the curriculum that I am expected to use	Be more enthusiastic when the schedule does not permit me to do what I want with my students
What positive actions can you take to help you monitor and achieve your personal goal?	I need to develop more effective strategies on how I respond to students negative questions about literacy tasks rather than just get annoyed with their questions	

Teaching Ideas for the Literacy Classroom

My Thoughts on Teaching Enthusiasm

Now you want to help your students be more enthusiastic about reading and writing. What can you do to help them achieve this goal?

How will you invite students to set individual goals to achieve Enthusiasm in Reading and Writing:

As I was doing the research for this chapter and discussing the goal of enthusiasm with other teachers, I learned that all it takes are a few small negative factors to increase frustration over time. For example, I know that it is important to have high-quality books in the classroom and I am certain most of the teachers I have taught also have this same belief, but when I visit the classrooms, I hear about their frustrations about a lack of resources. This propels a negative attitude with students about the lack of resources in the classroom. When teaching the behavior of enthusiasm for reading and writing with students find ways to have fun with literacy.

Having Fun with Hobbies

When I was a fourth grade teacher, I would share my love of American Girl Dolls and the books that accompanied them. To invite students into sharing their literacy hobbies with the class, I had them bring their hobby artifacts into the classroom. The purpose of the activity was to share my interests in reading and motivate them to become interested in other aspects of reading and writing by using hobbies as a theme. Photograph 2.1 shows the display I had in my room. I also integrated this activity with the novel we were reading in language arts.

Photograph 2.1 Sharing Literacy Hobbies

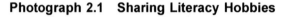

(Photo taken by Susan E. Israel)

Showing Support for Home-School-Community Connections

Many parents do not have time for reading. Because time is an issue, gaining access to literature might also be challenging for parents and students. You can show your enthusiasm for reading and writing, as well as increase home-school-community connections by inviting librarians to bring books into the classroom for students to check out and take home. Have the librarian bring extra library card applications to send home with the students. If you are focusing on a specific genre or theme in language arts, let the librarian know and invite her to bring print material on related topics. You can post *I Wish my Teacher Would Read* lists on your chalkboard and have students write down items they wish they could read. Send the wish list to the librarian.

I Wish My Teacher Would Read:

1. More books about animals

2. Comic books

3. Mystery books about historical people

Starbucks for Literacy

Host a book read-in at your local Starbucks. When I was visiting a local Starbucks, I noticed many thank you notes from students hanging on the walls. The students wrote notes to the manager thanking him for letting them spend time at his store to read their stories to customers. The students drew pictures on their thank you notes. Many of the students commented on how wonderful the free drinks were. I loved seeing those letters and I thought this was a wonderful way that the community can demonstrate enthusiasm for reading and writing. I noticed several stories that the students had written were also hanging on the wall. The manager really went above and beyond to share the Starbucks experience with students and make their experience into a literacy one.

Table 2.5　Literature that Promotes the Value of Reading

The Great Good Thing By Roderick Townley (2001). New York: Scholastic

Summer Reading is Killing Me! By Jon Scieszka (1998). A Puffin Book

The Bookstore Mouse By Peggy Christian (1995). Harcourt, Inc.

Who's Afraid of the Big Bad Book? By Lauren Child (2002). Hyperion Books for Children

I Love My Little Story Book By Anita Jeram (2002). Walker Books

The Classroom at the End of The Hall By Douglas Evans (1996). Front Street Books, Inc.

Hank Zipzer: The Mostly True Confessions of the World's Best Underachiever: I Got A "D" in Salami By Henry Winkler (2003). Grossett & Dunlap.

The quote by Katie at the beginning of this chapter is an inspiring thought for teachers who desire to exemplify enthusiasm in literacy instruction and helps teachers realize that the heart of the teacher is really the core essence of exemplary teachers who engage students in reading and writing. Teachers modeling enthusiasm in the classroom nurture students' love of reading and writing. Ultimately, this love for literacy will extend beyond the classroom.

Teachers Thinking Deeply

Following is a list of questions and professional development resources that are recommended to teachers who want to reflect deeply on their instructional practices in reading and writing.

Discussion Questions to Maintain and Extend Goal

1. Many educators might argue for rigor in their subject areas and higher standards, rather than enthusiasm for reading and writing, as central to their beliefs. Can we have both?

2. Teaching philosophy is reflected in teaching pedagogy. Does the concept of enthusiasm fit well with your own philosophy of teaching? How does this philosophy fit within the framework of your school and community?

3. Exemplary teachers display enthusiasm for reading and writing. Do you know any teachers who display this quality in their classrooms but not at the expense of high standards and rigor?

4. What can you learn from teachers who demonstrate enthusiasm for reading and writing?

Real-life Classroom Scenario

This student is a kindergarten boy named Joe. Joe is very bright and full of energy. Joe gets in trouble often for the way he treats other children. Joe needs to be challenged more in class. He always seems to be bored with the academics. When Joe is a helper he usually has a good day. What ideas do you have that would demonstrate your enthusiasm for his ability to be more motivated to learn?

Personal and Professional Literacy Resources

- *A Qualified Teacher in Every Classroom? Appraising Old Answers and New Ideas.* Edited by Frederick M. Hess, Andrew J. Rotherham, and Kate Walsh. (2004). Cambridge, MA: Harvard Educational Press. This book can be used to help teachers and administrators understand how qualified teachers exhibit behaviors of enthusiasm for reading and writing. This book can be used as an additional professional development resource when reading this book.

- *Adolescents Talk about Reading: Exploring Resistance to and Engagement With Text,* by Anne R. Reeves (2004). Newark, DE: International Reading Association. This resource focuses on how teachers can learn about the art and craft of teaching by listening to adolescent students engage in conversations about reading and writing.

- *Quotes to Inspire Great Reading Teachers,* C. C. Block and S. E. Israel (2006). Thousand Oaks, CA: Corwin Press. This resource can be used as a motivational tool for literacy teachers who want to reflect more deeply on research-based actions of exemplary teachers.

Goal #2: Unity

Teacher Creates Opportunities for All Learners

Teachers are responsible to accommodate each individual and their needs. Making sure there is a large variety of rich literature that interests each student. I want my students to feel valued with not only their reading but their writing too.

—Jacob, 5th Grade Teacher

Journaling Thoughts on Unity

To me, it is essential to have unity in your classroom before you can address the individual needs of each learner. If your class is not *united*, students may have difficulty feeling a sense of acceptance. What does the word unity mean to you in the context of your class and the larger school community? When I think about unity, I think about the union between one or more working toward a common goal. This chapter focuses on helping teachers achieve the goal of unity in their classroom and the larger school community. After reading this chapter, you will become more aware of how to create opportunities so that all learners, regardless of cultural barriers or learning disabilities, feel included. Because of the change in the varying levels of diversity, especially in regards to literacy ability, socio-cultural aspects, and social factors, teachers are finding it necessary to make adaptations relative to literacy opportunities.

Why do you want to make a commitment to the learning behavior of creating unity in the classroom? Do you believe the goal will have an influence on instruction?

Thoughts for Group Discussion:

Self-Reflection: Making a Commitment

Goal Rationale:

Regardless of ethnicity or color, all students have a constitutional right to learning opportunities. Being able to create an environment in which all learners are included can be a challenge regardless of the grade level. According the Standards outlined in the Introduction, creating opportunities for diverse learners also creates a learning environment based on acceptance. Exemplary teachers strive to create a classroom climate in which students unite and feel safe to learn.

To help overcome negative influences, research has addressed the increase in student diversity by responding to reforms relative to such populations as English language learners, social interactions, and bilingual and English as second language programs. Fitzgerald (2000) recommends literacy instruction focus on opportunities that are filled with multivoiced and muliliteracy opportunities. For example, teachers should consider the student's native language first and try to use a variety of literacies to make connections back to skill development in reading and writing.

Reform also focuses on increased levels of professional development for pre-service and in-service teachers in the area of improving the ability to provide instruction in a second language (Garcia, 2000; Jaménez & Barrera, 2000; Jaménez, Smith, & Martinex-León, 2003). More teachers are being required to learn second languages as well as specific strategies on how to teach diverse populations. Due to sociocultural factors, reform is also addressing issues of how social implications with the goal of closing the literacy gap between poorer and richer communities (Rogers, 2000).

Scripted curriculum is also a major issue that influences the delivery of instruction, therefore, without curriculum reform, more and more students will have fewer and fewer opportunities for social interactions (Purcell-Gates, 2000), which is important for unity with students to occur in the classroom. Exemplary literacy teachers create unity in their classrooms by meeting individual and developmental needs (Block, Oakar, & Hurt, 2002) clear discussions, student conferences, the ability to exercise flexibility, and time spent reteaching content in meaningful ways so as not to exclude or leave behind students who do not accelerate.

Multiliteracies also include the literacy of technology. Effective instruction includes utilization of technology to increase reading and writing not only in school, but also in the home community where many students desire to be part of the technological community. Therefore, access to technology for all students can no longer be ignored. According to Mahiri (2000), the ability to access knowledge using technology plays a role in how classrooms remain unified. If technology is not available for all students, then students who do not have or are not permitted to have access are unable to obtain knowledge. Knowledge sharing is what we do in school; this sharing is what builds community-establishing literacy unity. Based on the research, several negative factors have the potential to influence the type of literacy opportunities teachers can create for all learners.

The research on how we teach literacy to learners with special needs suggests that teachers first spend more time on developing professionally in the area of cultural diversity and learners with special needs, such as English language learners. Professional development should be the starting point and examining how unity is displayed in your classroom will provide the lens to better understand how to increase your knowledge on literacy instruction for these specific populations. To help you identify specific areas to develop, respond to the self-assessment below.

Achieving the literacy goal of unity is not an easy task for today's busy teachers. Many factors influence unity goal attainment. Raising awareness about negative factors that minimize a unified community will help teachers directly assess their own instructional behaviors keeping them from unity and meeting the needs of individual learners. Reflect on the list in Table 3.1 to identify any negative factors that have the potential to reduce unity in your classroom. Place a check by the negative factors that you experience as a teacher.

Table 3.1   Factors That Prevent Unity Checklist

_____ 1. Teachers having negative attitudes about receiving professional development to provide instruction in the student's home language.

_____ 2. School districts that adopt a *One size fits all* ideology with curricular engagements.

_____ 3. Teachers who feel they need to exercise control over students' learning all the time.

_____ 4. When students are not permitted to engage in discussion about literacy because the classroom or school philosophy is to maintain quiet classrooms, which minimize opportunities for oral language development and positive social interactions that promote unity.

_____ 5. Cultural awareness of students and the integration of their culture in the classroom curriculum.

_____ 6. Displaying student work that is not of high quality, therefore, deteriorating self-confidence in those whose work never is displayed.

_____ 7. Inadequate opportunities for how students internalize the value of learning about how social interactions can be influenced by language differences.

_____ 8. Not enough technology resources for all students, especially related to culturally specific software and technology tools.

Review the list and reflect on the negative factors you have checked. Do you notice any trends with your responses? Are their other factors that need to be considered when building unity in your classroom? Record your thoughts below.

_____

_____

_____

_____

_____

Observation from a Window into Literacy Lives

As an Assistant Professor, one of my responsibilities is to observe my pre-service teachers. One particular observation has always stood out when I think about how teachers' behaviors maximize or minimize learning for all students. The cooperating teacher was teaching on one side of the room and my student teacher was teaching a small group on the other side of the room. All but one of the students were sitting on the floor by each teacher. The student who was sitting in the back of the room had a learning disability. Part of the IEP plan was inclusion in the regular classroom with support. The student was a boy about eight years old. When I observed him, he had his hands crossed holding a pencil in one hand and his head resting on his arms. He was very frustrated for some reason. The teacher could not get him to do his work so she made him stand in the corner of the room. I about died when this happened. The boy must have felt so excluded from the group and most likely this distracted him from his work.

Think about students in your classroom who need assistance with learning? Have you ever experienced students acting out when they were not included in group activities? Why do you think they acted this way? How would you respond to this situation?

Self-questioning to Achieve Goal

Self-questioning to Achieve Goal

What challenges do you experience that keep you from demonstrating unity?

How Colleagues Overcome Challenges:

Did you identify with any of the negative factors above when thinking about how your opportunities for individual learners are created? What type of attributes do you associate with a teacher who promotes unity in the classroom? Do you recall a teacher or someone who made you feel included? The research reforms described above should help you reflect on what aspects in your classroom might contribute to a lack of unification.

Several real-life problems with research-based solutions are discussed below. It is my recommendation that while reading the problem-based narratives below, you focus your attention on the positive research-based solutions. As you read the problems and solutions below and reflect on the following questions:

- What did you learn from the checklist about your behaviors you display that demonstrate you create opportunities for unification?
- Do you see patterns emerging in your beliefs and specific problems generated by your beliefs?
- How might your beliefs influence how you address individual learners who need additional support in your classroom?
- What can you identify as a goal for yourself?
- How will you work toward the goal of unity in your classroom?

Now more than ever, literacy teachers are experiencing fewer and fewer classrooms with a homogeneous population. The diversity of the students presents teachers with issues that require a different way of teaching.

As a literacy professor, I am responsible for teaching pre-service and in-service teachers who are pursuing degrees in education and literacy. Around the second night of class, I like to hold informal discussion about the literacy issues or fears of teaching literacy they are currently dealing with in their classrooms. I do this to scaffold future lessons around issues that are important to the students in my class at the time. Some of the fears teachers face are listed below.

- How to effectively teach and include students who cannot read on grade level
- Dealing with frustrations about how much time it takes to work with individual students who lack literacy skills
- Trying to create opportunities for parent involvement when there is a lack of parental support to being with
- Teaching from curriculum materials that teachers are mandated to use
- Effective approaches to teaching non-English speaking students

Increasing Opportunities for Social Interactions

During silent reading time, students are expected to be reading books of their choosing. Some students do utilize this precious time wisely, many more tend to keep themselves looking busy reading. Students with special needs have difficulty reading independently and non-English students do not have access to books from their own culture or written in their own language so they tend to benefit the least from any time given for sustained silent reading.

Jaménez, Smith, and Martinex-León, (2003) studied language and literacy practices in two Mexican schools. In order to understand the language and literacy practices in these schools, they wanted to understand the ideologies of reading and writing. What they discovered was a difference in the tolerance for oral language. Mexican students had freedom to talk and express themselves orally. Teachers in the schools allowed them to do so without constantly worrying about noise being generated. This study is valuable to reading instruction because teachers should now understand the value of oral language for culturally diverse students. Instead of having sustained silent reading all the time, teachers should acknowledge the cultural values of non-English speaking children by having sustained social reading (SSR). SSR gives diverse learners opportunities to share information about the books they are reading, as well as learn from others' discussions about text.

GOAL OF LESSON: Think critically about choice text by participating in Sustained Social Reading time.

METHOD FOR INSTRUCTION: Have students group themselves with common books they are reading. Students can talk with students to find out more about the books and eventually form small discussion groups.

DISCUSSION STRATEGIES: Teachers can post discussion questions on the board and explain the procedures students should follow. Three procedures that can be followed are:

1. Learn about the books being read by the students in your small group.
2. Understand why peers are reading a particular book.
3. Discuss freely key concepts or ideas in the book and how they related to real-life situations.

DEVELOPING THE DISPOSTION: Understanding how different cultures view written and spoken language can influence approaches to literacy instruction. Creating an opportunity for students to freely discuss books creates a climate in which students are united by books.

Obtaining Teaching Resources for Individual Learning Needs

When students do not have access to books and technological resources, teachers feel a sense of frustration. The availability of teaching resources for all learners decreases the number of effective instructional opportunities for literacy learning.

Not having adequate opportunities to obtain knowledge is a social injustice. Neuman and Celano (2006) conducted a large-scale ecological study in an urban community where teachers and students lacked adequate resources. Looking for answers, Neuman and Celano turned to the community to provide support. Their project, called the Model Urban Library initiative, created opportunities for poor children to have access to books and computers through increased funding. Based on the findings, libraries in urban communities became a place where the community and students were united by the goal of increasing reading achievement by providing higher quality resources for poor children.

A disappointing finding in the study was poor children do not know how to utilize library resources so they can benefit from them. Poorer children were in libraries while unattended and receiving little parental attention. Children visiting libraries in higher-socio-economic communities were accompanied by their parents as opposed to being dropped off with no supervision. In addition, their parents helped them select and use the library resources to gain knowledge, whereas parents in lower socio-economic communities used the library as a place to drop off their children. One interesting observation by the researchers that was making a difference regarding how students obtained information was from the actions of the urban librarian. The librarian assisted students in the following ways:

- Provided mentoring on book selections
- Interacted with the children when helping them select materials
- Started clubs based on interest and integrated literacy
- Provided informal instruction and guidance as needed
- Promoted a higher quality use of the libraries' resources
- Provided opportunities with technology with the purpose of obtaining knowledge and not game playing

Teachers can learn from this study by taking the following actions:

1. Provide parents with strategies to help students use the library resources.
2. Encourage parents to stay with their children in the library and provide informal instruction as needed.
3. Work with the librarians in impoverished communities to motivate them to change how they work with children.

Working With Parents to Increase Knowledge on English as Second Language (ESL) Learners

Teachers today are not adequately prepared to deal with the changing culture of the students. More training is necessary to understand how to teach ESL learners. Parents can also offer support for the teacher. Parents and teachers can work together with the school to engage in ongoing professional development related to English Language Learners. Following are several instructional strategies that can effectively help ESL learners are based on the recommendations from Drucker (2003). These same strategies can be shared with parents.

- Provide greater context for books being read by previewing the text in detail prior to reading.
- Repeated reading will provide more opportunities for ESL learners to internalize information.
- Invite students to participate in shared reading opportunities. Teachers can read with students using big books.
- Pair ESL learners with skilled readers and read portions of the text together.
- Choose texts that match the cultural schemata of the child.
- Have available a variety of reading materials in the classroom that represent many different cultures.
- Vocabulary integrated with text read. Permit students to write meanings of words in the margins or use Post-it notes.
- Sing vocabulary words paired with sign language or motion.
- Permit students to use their native languages when necessary.

Creating opportunities for literacy learning that builds unity creates a climate conducive to positive social interaction with all students. Identify problems and possible solutions in your classroom by responding to the following statements. Table 3.2 is a student inventory that can be administered. Adults can assist younger children by writing down their responses.

Table 3.2   Teacher Unity Inventory

Directions: Circle the response that best explains your belief about your teacher. Comments may be added to explain your response.

I believe that my teachers should give me an opportunity to share freely stories about our culture and traditions.

       Strong Belief   Occasionally Value   Room for Growth

I believe that my teacher should support all students by allowing them to engage in peer reviews.

       Strong Belief   Occasionally Value   Room for Growth

I believe that I deserve instruction that builds both the skill and desire to read increasingly complex materials.

       Strong Belief   Occasionally Value   Room for Growth

I understand the value of oral language and reading aloud in my classroom is important.

       Strong Belief   Occasionally Value   Room for Growth

I believe parents are of value; therefore, parents should help in the classroom when they are available.

       Strong Belief   Occasionally Value   Room for Growth

I believe that social interactions in the classroom should be limited during silent reading time.

       Strong Belief   Occasionally Value   Room for Growth

I believe that conversations and discussions during class and instruction are disruptive for all learners.

       Strong Belief   Occasionally Value   Room for Growth

I believe that I should have an opportunity to share my concerns about unity with our class.

       Strong Belief   Occasionally Value   Room for Growth

Challenges in my classroom that influence my ability to provide opportunities for unity in my classroom are:

_____

_____

_____

_____

_____

Effective actions I can take to create opportunities for all learners:

_____

_____

_____

_____

_____

Self-evaluation of Progress

Self-evaluation of Progress

Have you achieved your goal? If not, what positive action can you take to achieve the goal?

New Ideas:

This chapter concentrated on helping teachers achieve unity in their classrooms and in the larger school community. The goals of this chapter were:

- Create learning opportunities for all learners, which include students with diverse backgrounds, English language learners, minorities, at-risk students, and students with special needs.

- Provide meaningful learning opportunities in a climate that is sensitive to supporting the social and emotional development of all learners.

- Utilize opportunities and resources available in the larger school community to assist in providing effective learning outcomes for all learners.

Unity builds community. Think about the students in your classroom. How do diverse learners feel? Do all students feel a sense of unity? Identify students with whom you would like to work so they feel more included in literacy learning in your classroom.

When formulating a plan to achieve the literacy goal of unity, keep in mind the following behaviors:

- Provide oral language opportunities for diverse students

- Create moments when students are interacting with literacy

- Work with parents and the larger school community to make literacy resources available

- Invite parents of at-risk students to work with you on learning strategies to effectively mentor their child in libraries

- Seek out opportunities to learn effective strategies on how to teach diverse learners

 My personal literacy goal to bring unity and create learning opportunities for all learners in my classroom is

_____

_____

_____

_____

_____

_____

_____

_____

_____

_____

The reason this goal is important to me is:

_____

_____

_____

_____

_____

_____

_____

Self-monitoring Checklist

Self-monitoring Statement	Behaviors you Display	Changes you Need to Make
What new actions did you take to create learning opportunities for all learners?		
How did you encourage students who are learning to speak English?		
What did you do differently related to your instructional goals to help you include special needs students so they feel part of the larger class community?		
How did you change the physical environment so that students have an opportunity to work together in a unified manner?		
Did you consider the background of your students when addressing the learning climate in your classroom?		
Did you identify ways to be sensitive to students who might have social or emotional needs?		
Did the students have an opportunity to discuss and make recommendations to develop a climate that supports unity in your classroom?		
Did you achieve your personal literacy goal that you wrote about at the beginning of this chapter? How did you achieve your goal?		

My Self-monitoring Checklist

Self-monitoring Statement	Behaviors you Display	Changes you Need to Make
What new actions did you take to create learning opportunities for all learners?	I like to divide my class into small groups on the first day of class and let students share with me their talents	I need to evaluate how I communicate assignments to me students with are ELL
How did you encourage students who are learning to speak English?	Use a peer group to help monitor progress and explain information in a different way	Work more closely with parents to ensure we communicate in an effective manner
What did you do differently related to your instructional goals to help you include special needs students so they feel part of the larger class community?	I do not let my inclusion students sit alone with their IEP instructor	I need to make sure I share literacy resources that focus on special needs
How did you change the physical environment so that students have an opportunity to work together in a unified manner?	I create many different spaces around the room for small groups to work together	I need to make sure I am sensitive to students who need to work with other students who can help them translate
Did you identify ways to be sensitive to students who might have social or emotional needs?		I need to learn more about social and emotional needs of children
What behaviors you display related to your literacy goal that have been effective?	Spending more time with individual students who have special needs and learning about how I can help them	Watching how I respond to students who are struggling when I am having a bad day

Teaching Ideas for the Literacy Classroom

My Thoughts on Teaching Unity

Now you want to help your students display the behavior of unity. What can you do in your classroom, during collaborative activities, and at recess?

How will you intive students to set individual goals to achieve unity?

Literacy Fear Factor

To achieve the goal of unity to create opportunities for individual and diverse learners, provide time for students to discuss their fears about literacy learning. Divide the class into two small groups. I have found that students seem to be more open to discussion when there are fewer opportunities for peer pressures. Have younger students draw pictures of their fears. Invite older students to make a list. Because time always seems to be a factor, I set aside twenty minutes for a Literacy Fear Factor Discussion. Give students five minutes to write down their fears about literacy. When students are done, spend the next ten minutes sharing the fears. Give students opportunities to explain why they have fears and how it might influence their learning. While students are sharing their fears with the group, I am making a list of their comments. I also ask one older student to make a list with me. When everyone has shared their fears, I give students time to brainstorm solutions on how they can overcome their fears. The last part of class is spent discussing their solutions.

Around the World Literacy Presentations

To avoid putting students who struggle with English in positions where they have to give presentations in front of the entire class, I place students in small groups of four of five when working on projects that require a presentation. One of my requirements is that the group begin the presentation as a group. When presenting their material or content learned, individual students need to present to a smaller group of students rather than the entire class. When all the presentations are done, I expect the group to bring the class back together for closing comments. I expect the students who were listening to the presentations to share two positive thoughts about what they learned and one suggestion on something they wished they would have learned or would like to learn in the future. My rationale for having students present material to smaller groups is to create classroom unity and to avoid making students who do not speak well in front of their peers embarrassed. Thinking about how students give presentations is one way of thinking differently about building unity in the classroom. The following guidelines are provided to the students before they begin planning for large and small group presentations.

Title of Presentation:

Group Members:

Guidelines:

1. Begin your presentation as a larger group. Introduce your topic and your reason for selecting the topic. Give students an overview of what you will present in smaller groups. Divide students into four or five groups depending on how many students are presenting. Each student will present to a small group.

2. Small groups will listen to the presentation and rotate once completely so that all groups get an opportunity to listen to the presentations.

---

3. When presentations are done, return to the larger classroom groups.

4. As a group, provide the larger group with closing comments. This can include what you have learned or enjoyed about your presentation.

5. Ask students to give you feedback on your presentation in the form of two positive comments and one suggestion for future topics to learn.

Over the years, I have learned that having students work in smaller groups is an effective way to create unity in the classroom. In addition, I try to end classroom discussions on positive notes by inviting students to share positive comments with the entire class. Students who lack confidence or feel they are not part of a group will benefit greatly when they get to hear positive comments about themselves in front of their peers. This is a huge motivator in the classroom!

Unity brings all learners together and provides them with equal opportunities for literacy learning. You became more sensitive to students by providing them with social literacy opportunities to help them be a part of the "whole" class. One of my favorite bulletin boards is in Photograph 3.1. The reason I like this photo is because the teacher is displaying a belief that all students are in a community of readers.

Photograph 3.1

(Photo taken in EDU 601: Phonics, Spelling, and Word Studies by Susan E. Israel at the University of Dayton)

Unification in the classroom and in the community provides harmony, which influences learning and motivation. In the next chapter, your literacy goal to achieve is kindness. This disposition focuses on behaviors that will provide positive literacy engagements in a classroom where the teacher is now enthusiastic about literacy and has unity within the core school class and community.

Teachers Thinking Deeply

Following is a list of questions and professional development resources that are recommended to teachers who want to reflect deeply on their instructional practices and create environments in which all students can learn regardless of individual needs.

Discussion Questions to Maintain and Extend Goal

1. What problems do you face in your classroom that keep you from creating a unified learning environment?

2. Does the concept of unity exist within your teaching philosophy? If so, how? If not, how can you change this behavior so that all students feel included?

3. Recall an experience when a student in your classroom felt he or she was part of the group and told you so? How did this make you feel? What prompted this student to communicate feelings about unity?

4. Many educators face the dilemma of getting students involved. What does parental involvement have to do with unity? How can you create a community of parent volunteers? What strategies can you suggest for making this happen?

5. Several recent research-based solutions were presented in this chapter. Based on the research, what instructional changes will you make to increase unity and meet the needs of individual learners?

6. How often do students in your classroom engage in oral discourse? What observations do you notice when students are working with their peers? How do you make adaptations for students who are not as comfortable expressing their thoughts in a group situation?

Real-life Classroom Scenario

Maya is a struggling reader in the first grade. She moved to the United States with her parents when she was four years old. Her parents understand little English at all. Maya has picked up the language but has a lot of trouble pronouncing words correctly. When reading, she often has trouble making beginning letter sounds, and she has little comprehension. She also has little confidence as a reader. What can you do to increase both Maya's comprehension as well as her confidence?

Personal and Professional Literacy Resources

Following is a list of resources that I have used to become more knowledgeable in the area of teaching diverse learners.

- Gutiérrez, K. D. et al. (2002). "Sounding American": The consequences of new reforms on English language learners. *Reading Research Quarterly, 37, 328-343.* This article outlines research-based strategies that will benefit those working with non-English speaking children.

- Kozol, J. (2005). *The shame of the nation: Restoration of apartheid schooling in America.* New York: Crown Publishers. This resource discusses aspects of social and economic forces in America, which has always been an underlying factor related to successful public and private educational systems. Use this research to help you develop a more global understanding of economic diversity.

- Malloy, E. A. (1992). *Culture and commitment: The challenges of today's universities.* Notre Dame, IN: University of Notre Dame Press. What I like about this book are the personal stories that professors share about teaching experiences that have shaped their beliefs and cultural development.

Goal #3: Kindness

Teacher Maintains
a Positive Literacy Environment

"Children are not the people of tomorrow, but are people of today. They have a right to be taken seriously, and to be treated with tenderness and respect. They should be allowed to grow into whoever they were meant to be. The unknown person inside each of them is our hope for the future."

—Janusz Korczak, Physician, teacher, and writer.

(Quote from Ten Amazing People: And How They Changed the World, Shaw, 2003)

Journaling Thoughts on Kindness

In the first two chapters of this book, you have read observations from my teaching journals about memorable teachers or experiences that have made a difference in how I teach. To attain the goal of kindness, I want to share an excerpt from a letter that I received from one of my graduate students. I am not sharing this letter to make myself look good, but instead, to make you think differently. This letter helped me realize that actions of kindness make a difference in people's lives.

Why do you want to make a commitment to the learning behavior of kind-ness? Why will achieving this goal have an influence on instruction?

Thoughts for Group Discussion:

Dr. Israel,

Just a quick note to say "hi" and share a couple of things with you. First of all, per your request, I have enclosed a copy of my personal reflection journal in response to the book entitled, *Comprehension* by Gretchen Owacki. I truly appreciated all of your comments and the resources you placed inside of it. I wanted to thank you for a couple of things, and at the same time apologize for just now getting around to it. As we go through life, we cross paths with many people and as time goes on some are remembered and some are forgotten. I will think of you often…for the great many things you taught me. Yes…no doubt about it I learned a lot about issues, trends, and research and I am very grateful for that. However, I am even more grateful for the things that you gave me. It may have been a small thing, but the list you compiled sharing everyone's thoughts in regards to what's right about teaching is very meaningful to me. I have it framed at home and I look at it often. I think about the video you showed us and on the days when it seems nothing is going right, I stop and reflect on the message you left me with. It has changed the way I think and it has changed how I respond to the challenges I am presented with.

I also want to let you know how much it meant to find the old postcard in the journal. It was so nice of you to share your collection with me, and even though initially you told me I could take one. I didn't feel right in doing so. It was quite a surprise to find it in the book, and I will always keep it.

Finally, thank you ever so much for the lovely writing journal you presented me with on the last evening of class. I was absolutely amazed that you took the time to find a book for every person in the class, chosen specifically for that person. It made me realize just how much you really knew each person in the class.

> —The letter was signed by the student and the
> salutation read, From the Heart.
> (Israel, 2004, Personal Communication).

What lessons can you learn from this letter? What can you learn about the acts of kindness I did to motivate my students? What I learned about myself is that people value acts of kindness, even the smallest ones.

Self-Reflection: Making a Commitment

What do actions of kindness look like in your classroom? What type of characteristics do you believe kind teachers possess? Why is it important to be kind to our students, as well as to the larger school community? What does kindness mean to you? When I type kindness into my computer and search for related synonyms, I find the following words that are similar to kindness:

- compassion
- gentleness

- sympathy
- kindheartedness
- thoughtfulness
- consideration

Did you use any of these synonyms to describe the kind teacher you were thinking of? This chapter focuses on helping teachers achieve the goal of kindness by learning how to maintain a positive classroom. Teachers will reflect on how kindness is embedded into the daily happenings of the school day and learn new methods on how to integrate kindness in literacy practices.

Early reading researchers (Israel & Monaghan, 2007) believe that student achievement and motivation are guided by the actions of the teacher; actions of kindness.

Dewey, father of progressivism, believed kindness permeated through the teachers into the students.

> When the school introduces and trains each child of society into membership within such a little community, saturating him with the spirit of service, and providing him with the instruments of effective self-direction, we shall have the deepest and best guaranty of a larger society which is worthy, lovely, and harmonious. (Dewey, 1902, 2001, p. 20)

Dewey's progressive way of thinking supported instruction that focused on the individual student and his or her needs. Dewey encouraged his teachers to understand the interests of the students they are teaching and focus practices on those interests. Kindness was enveloped in the actions of teachers when the students were given opportunities to utilize their experiences outside of school within in the school setting. Kindness was also demonstrated when the teachers were sympathetic of the child's own instincts, allowing him or her to be involved in fundamental school decision making.

More recently reading researchers are looking at identity construction in readers and writers. McCarthey's (2001) review of the literature also supports that teacher attitudes and behaviors affect learning and motivation. To me, the most disturbing outcome important for teachers to know is, literacy experiences affect attitudes in students. Poorer readers reported having the highest level of negativism toward literacy. Identity construction focuses on shifting attention away from self and toward the direction of a construct found in social, cultural, and historical contexts. This is better explained by McCarthey who states, "we are shaped by how the world sees us" (p. 125). A question that you might be asking and one that I would like you to reflect on in relationship to you and your teaching situation is, what teaching actions positively or negatively influence how my students view themselves? How will the disposition of kindness influence student learning and motivation?

Another major study, conducted by Pressley and his research team, investigated "whole" school effects in 14 classrooms on literacy achievement (Pressley, 2006). In this study, he found the school produced consistently high reading achievement scores. His preliminary findings concluded that the best instruction found in the best classrooms within the school have exceptionally positive environments. He can safely state that the school as a whole is never negative about anything. Pressley records the following thoughts in his analysis, "There is little failure, with students receiving supportive instruction that encourages them to grow from where they are at present, rather than be frustrated that they are not at some attainable standard for them" (Pressley, 2006, p. 5).

In effective classrooms for decades we find effective teachers who have attained the goal of kindness by maintaining positive literacy environments. What behaviors do effective teachers in exceptionally positive environments possess? What does literacy instruction look like in these classrooms, as opposed to substandard negative ones? Issues or negative factors prohibiting the teacher from exhibiting a kind disposition include those listed in Table 4.1.

Table 4.1 Factors That Minimize Teacher's Ability to Display Kindness Checklist

_____	1. Overload of teacher expectations because of larger classroom size
_____	2. Overwhelming amount of paper grading due to standards integration
_____	3. School mandates based on curriculum reform
_____	4. Insufficient resources due to a lack of funding
_____	5. Personal issues that cause instructional distractions
_____	6. Disconnect with school community and culture

(Continued on next page)

Table 4.1   Factors That Minimize Teacher's Ability to Display Kindness Checklist *(Continued)*

_____	7. Disciplinary problems with students who struggle with academics
_____	8. Strained patience due to inclusion of students with special needs
_____	9. Lack of administrative support
_____	10. A lack of teacher knowledge of teaching literacy with at-risk or challenging student
_____	11. Other factors

Review the list and reflect on the factors you have checked. Do you notice any trends with your responses? Are there other factors that you should consider? If so, what will you do to address these concerns?

_____

_____

_____

_____

_____

_____

_____

_____

_____

_____

_____

_____

Self-questioning to Achieve Goal

Self-questioning to Achieve Goal

What challenges do you experience that keep you from demonstrating kindness?

How Colleagues Overcome Challenges:

Attaining the goal of kindness does not take a lot of time. It only takes enough time to rethink your own disposition about issues or concerns that are causing you to be unkind. By rethinking your own personal and instructional objectives, you can find ways to demonstrate to students' kindness. There are so many variables that teachers are bombarded with that reaching the goal of kindness on different days or during different situations seems impossible. Every teacher has the inner ability to possess genuine caring (Sanacore, 2004). I think that negative experiences in the classroom distract teachers from their own inner spirit that they lose sight of who they really are. It is my hope that by reading stories about other situations, you might rediscover the kind teacher you are or want to be. Below you will read about problems that get in the way of teacher kindness. As you read, make a list of your own ideas of what you can learn from these experiences.

Generating Happiness by Making Changes

Students seem to generate a lot of inner anxiety about tests and test taking. Are you tired of having to show kindness when testing is not a pleasant experience? Consider giving a choice on taking a test or doing something else that is more relevant to students needs: Think long and hard about evaluation and consider alternative formats for all the different learning styles of your students. For example, give students five essay questions and ask them to pick three. Instead of giving a mandatory final, offer a service project and a written summary.

Disruptive students not only cause problems for the teacher but they also keep others from learning. Attention might be a cause of a student misbehaving in class. You can demonstrate kindness with difficult students by changing the way you respond to them. Be unique and do something for your students that no other teachers can do or is doing: What can you do for your students that demonstrates your gratitude for their presence in your classes? Here are a few suggestions:

- Communicate procedures and expectations in advance
- Develop an early rapport with parents and students to cultivate a positive relationship prior to any negative experience
- Do not interrogate or humiliate your students in front of their peers
- Find ways to distract misbehavior through lively discussions
- Provide students with opportunities to interact with peers to foster a love of reading that encourages positive, peer-collaborative relationships
- Use journaling as a technique with students who desire more of your attention and respond to journals promptly

To help my graduate students think differently about their experiences as a teacher and avoid the pitfall of always focusing on negative school-related experiences, I shared with my students on the last day of class a video called, *Celebrating What's Right about the World* by Dewitt Jones. I credit a colleague of mine, Bill Losito, from the University of

Dayton for introducing me to this video. If you have not seen that video, I highly recommend you watch it or use it in your classroom to learn how to view the world from different perspectives.

I titled my presentation, *Celebrate What's Right about Teaching.* The reason I showed the video was that I had a group of graduate students who always talked about the issues they face in the classroom. Unfortunately, my graduate students seemed to incubate a negative disposition over the course of the semester about all the issues they faced in teaching. I did not want the students to focus on everything negative about teaching; therefore, I asked them to reflect on the things that they think are right about teaching. I have included a version of that poem that we wrote as a class in Figure 4.1 in case you are interested in reading it. On the original version, I placed the student's name after the thing he or she identified as being important to him or her about teaching.

Celebrate What's Right about Teaching!

Students learning. The way they make you feel
    when they finally understand. Team teaching—
    the great ideas and friendships you make.
Seeing the students light up when they understand
    something.
Getting notes that say: 'You are the best teacher in
    the *hole* world!'
How the kids love you!
Helping struggling learners see good in themselves
    —believing in who they are.
You have the opportunity to love and be loved by
    many little people!
Loving your students and treating them as you
    would your own children.
When the "light" goes on—when the student gets it!

Figure 4.1 Class poem based on the theme, Celebrate What's Right about Teaching *(Inspired by a video narrated by Dewitt Jones)*

Making a difference. Seeing smiles. Being a positive role model. Great colleagues. Having a job where I feel independent and can be creative.

The most exciting shift in teaching that I've seen is the focus on teaching reading with a concentration on processing.

Wonderful professional literature.

We teach them to read, a skill they will use for the rest of their lives.

I love using computers to help my kids write.

You can take a child at any level and see them learning and taking shape.

It's not a dead-end job. There are so many opportunities for learning—for developing professionally as an educator.

Motivation from our peers and students when we all get it!

Always having something to laugh about.

Teachers wanting to learn more and expand their level of thinking.

Summers off.

Figure 4.1   Class poem based on the theme, Celebrate What's Right about Teaching *(Inspired by a video narrated by Dewitt Jones) (Continued)*

Five lessons I want you to learn about kindness as it relates to teaching from the heart and the behaviors of exemplary literacy teachers after reading the letter from my graduate student and reflecting on the poem about *Celebrating What's Right about Teaching:*

Lesson #1: Show Genuine Interest
Get to know your students and in some way, respond to what you have learned about them during class and in small discussion groups.

Lesson #2: Develop an Attitude of Gratitude

Be grateful to your students for the kind things they do in the classroom for you and for others. Send them random notes when you notice kindness. Invite your students to also develop the attitude of gratitude by writing kind notes to classmates and other teachers in the school.

Lesson #3: Celebrate Success

Find ways to celebrate what is right about learning and school, and share your thoughts frequently with your students and their parents. Invite your administration to also share kind words with the students throughout the course of the year. For example, if someone compliments you on a project or an assignment, invite him or her to come to your class and tell your students personally.

Lesson #4: Developing Habits of Kindness

Frequently reflect on ways that you are integrating the disposition of kindness in your classroom. Encourage students to support actions of kindness. Avoid thinking and talking negatively all the time about your students in public places, like the teacher's lounge. One example of developing a habit of kindness is to place a marker board by your class door and every morning write a kind phrase about your class on the marker board. For example, you might write:

Marvelous 4th Graders Welcome to Monkey Monday

Terrific 2nd Graders Welcome to Tremendous Learning Tuesday

Lesson #5: Pre-planning for Teaching Success

You are the only person in your classroom who knows what is coming next related to lessons, activities, assessments, and scheduling. Think about what actions will influence your behaviors in advance and develop preplanning strategies on how to overcome and avoid being in situations that will cause you to be negative. For example, if noise bothers you during literature circles then have a parent sign-up sheet at back-to-school night and invite parents to monitor literature circle groups in the classroom or in another location in the school. I have found that sending small groups to different locations in the school helps create smaller group learning opportunities and decreases the level of noise in the classroom at any given time.

Now that you have learned about certain factors that might minimize behaviors of kindness in your classroom, take a few minutes to administer the Teacher Kindness Inventory with your students. Table 4.2 provides an example for you to use.

Table 4.2   Teacher Kindness Inventory

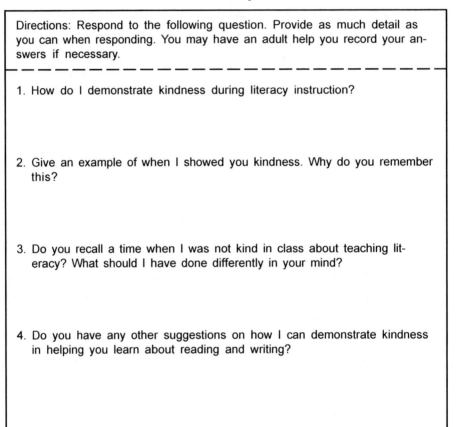

Directions: Respond to the following question. Provide as much detail as you can when responding. You may have an adult help you record your answers if necessary.

1. How do I demonstrate kindness during literacy instruction?

2. Give an example of when I showed you kindness. Why do you remember this?

3. Do you recall a time when I was not kind in class about teaching literacy? What should I have done differently in your mind?

4. Do you have any other suggestions on how I can demonstrate kindness in helping you learn about reading and writing?

Use the information you have learned from the *Teacher Kindness Inventory* to help you identify how your students feel about your behaviors of kindness. Do not worry or be offended if students point out something to you that is negative. That is only natural. I can tell you that it always takes me several weeks to look over my teaching evaluations. I am not sure why this is, only that criticism is very difficult for me to accept. I take teaching and my work as a teacher very seriously and I am always amazed how students perceive teaching actions differently. When one person thinks you are demonstrating an act of kindness another student in the same class might think you are showing favoritism toward a fellow classmate. When this happens, I have learned to seek clarification on what my students are telling me.

Learn from your students with the goal of achieving kindness. Permit them the opportunity to share with you their thoughts and always invite them to make recommendations for improvement. While reading something in a doctor's office once, I remember an article about change and how change is good because it gets us closer to perfection. Your goal is to be an exemplary literacy teacher; therefore, you will have to allow yourself to change.

 Now it is your turn to identify specific problems you are facing in your classroom that influence your ability to display kindness. You can also use this opportunity to discuss your feelings with peers who might be reading along with you.

Challenges in my classroom that negatively influence my ability to display kindness are:

_____
_____
_____
_____
_____
_____
_____
_____
_____
_____

Positive solutions to display kindness for all learners:

_____
_____
_____
_____
_____
_____
_____
_____
_____
_____

Self-evaluation of Progress

Self-evaluation of Progress

Have you achieved your goal? If not, what positive action can you take to achieve the goal?

New Ideas:

The literacy goal of this chapter focused on the helping teachers who work with children learn how the behavior of kindness is woven into daily literacy practices and how kindness influences students' motivation and learning. To help you realize the literacy goal of kindness, this chapter provided self-reflection and self-assessment to guide teacher actions on the following:

- Learn how to maintain a positive literacy environment while simultaneously avoiding negative thinking and negative decision making with students and the larger school community.

- Become aware of research-based practices that emphasize kindness in regard to literacy practices and to develop an appreciation for how exemplary literacy teachers use the behavior of kindness to create a motivating literacy experience for all children.
- Reflect on teacher acts of kindness so as to model them in your own practice and to integrate kindness in literacy curriculum planning throughout the school year.

Before identifying your own literacy goal that will help you actualize kindness in an aspect that you feel needs to be addressed, reflect on the following words of encouragement from Palmer:

> Good teaching is an act of hospitality toward the young, and hospitability is always an act that benefits the host even more than the guest. The concept of hospitality arose in ancient times when this reciprocity was easier to see…By offering hospitality, one participates in the endless reweaving of a social fabric on which all can depend—thus the gift of sustenance for the guest becomes a gift of hope for the host. It is that way in teaching as well: the teacher's hospitality to the student results in a world more hospitable to the teacher. (1998, p. 50)

What I like about Palmer's insight about hospitality is his association with the qualities of good teaching. What I learn from this quote as I reflect on good teaching qualities are the following:

- Kindness is a behavior that an exemplary teacher possesses and exhibits during the course of the day and the school year.
- Students are the guest at the literacy banquet and should be treated hospitably no matter what.
- Social fabric in the classroom is the culture or community that good teachers value and see kindness as a civil duty on one's literacy journey.
- Kindness becomes manifested in the culture of the classroom with reciprocity in turn benefiting the teacher.
- It is certain that exemplary teachers would not demonstrate an act of hospitality or kindness with the goal of benefiting themselves but do so because of their love of teaching from the heart and their love of children. Nonetheless, the truth remains that kindness begets kindness.
- Think differently about what kindness means in your teaching and how you can benefit from your own behavior of kindness.
- Kindness is one of the most inexpensive literacy tools of a teacher.

My personal literacy goal that will allow me to display kindness as a teacher is:

_____

_____

_____

_____

_____

_____

_____

_____

_____

_____

_____

The reason this goal is important to me is:

_____

_____

_____

_____

_____

_____

_____

_____

_____

_____

_____

When you reflect on how you demonstrate kindness to your students, how do you feel? What actions do you need to change to maintain a positive environment in the classroom? What did you learn from your students and your peers about kindness in a reading and writing classroom? How can you receive this information to obtain your literacy goal of kindness? Use the following self-monitoring checklist to see if you are achieving the literacy goal of kindness.

Self-monitoring Checklist

Self-Monitoring Statement	Behaviors you Display	Literacy or Behavioral Changes to Make
What actions are effective to maintaining a positive literacy environment?		
How are you kind to students you do not like?		
When you are unhappy with a mandated curriculum, what is your classroom behavior like?		
How do you act with students who are struggling readers?		
What literacy materials do you make available for students during silent reading or writing time?		

Self-monitoring Checklist

Self-Monitoring Statement	Behaviors you Display	Literacy or Behavioral Changes to Make
What actions are effective to maintaining a positive literacy environment?	Inviting students to donate their favorite books to my classroom library	Not telling children they cant read a book because it is too big or too hard
How are you kind to students you do not like?	I try to demonstrate kindness in the same manner regardless of the student	Watch who I let sit near me because sometimes I place students farther away from me if they bother me too much
When you are unhappy with a mandated curriculum, what is your classroom behavior like?		Avoid negative comments about what we are learning
How do you act with students who are struggling readers?	Not always pair students based on ability	Have conferences with students about how my actions impact their confidence
What literacy materials do you make available for students during silent reading or writing time?		I could let students read or write in special places rather than making them sit in their seat

Teaching Ideas for the Literacy Classroom

My Thoughts on Teaching Kindness

Now you want to help your students to develop behaviors of kindness. What can you do to help them achieve this goal?

How will you invite students to set individual goals to achieve Enthusiasm in Reading and Writing:

Teachers face many experiences throughout the course of the day that challenge maintaining a positive disposition at all times. By reflecting on your own literacy practices in regard to your disposition of kindness, change can occur. After you identify specific behaviors that cause you to not demonstrate kindness, potential solutions can be generated on how to address behaviors. I have found that if I think about my procedures and the motivation behind them in advance, I can minimize my changing behaviors over the course of a day. In other words, by careful assessment of my actions, it is easier to find ways to demonstrate kindness in advance rather than when it is too late. If you have not already done so, take a moment and congratulate yourself on the numerous ways you show kindness in your classroom so that student learning and motivation will tend to increase.

To achieve the goal of kindness to maintain a positive classroom environment you can consider implementing some of the following in your daily teaching routines.

Use Positive Language When Responding to Students

Deliver high expectations using positive language, such as "I am excited to share this information with you," or "We are going to celebrate..." During classroom discussions teachers face decisions about who to call on. I am guilty at times of making sure I call on a student who knows the right answer. I try to call on students who struggle when I am certain they have the right answer or at least a response that will not embarrass them in front of their peers. There are several strategies teachers can use when calling on students (Block, 2001). When students respond to a question with a wrong answer to a question, teachers can respond positively by saying the following:

1. *Reflect Further or Think Again.* Teachers can use this response when students are close to the right answer but just need more time to reconsider their response.

2. *That is the correct answer for this question.* Provide students with a new question that has their response as being correct. To keep them on track, give them the answer to your question again, and invite them to think of a question for the answer.

3. *I never thought of that.* Give students an opportunity to realize their ideas are valued. Try to explain how their response helps you reconsider your question.

4. *Let me elaborate further.* Avoid pointing out to students they have the wrong answer. Instead, respond by letting them know that you did not provide them with enough information to answer the question correctly.

5. *Help me understand your response.* Ask students to clarify their response in more detail. If you are still unclear about the response, invite students in smaller groups to reconsider the question and the answer. Sometimes students might have interpreted the question differently or did not really understand what you were asking. Give them an opportunity to explain their answer.

Welcoming Signs

When I was a fourth grade teacher, I posted a marker board by the front entrance of the classroom. Each morning I would post kind words about student achievements the prior day. Sometimes I would write silly welcoming phrases like Welcome to Wonderful Wednesday or Today is Terrific Tuesday. Eventually my students would take over writing kind phrases each morning. Another visible sign that demonstrates your kindness for your students and guests is placing a welcome mat by your door or desk. The welcome mat makes students feel invited into the learning experience from the moment they step into your classroom.

My Favorite Work Display

Frequently display all children's work and highlight what they have done well. For example, Photograph 4.1 shows how one teacher always displays all the students' work in the classroom and not just a few good pieces from the best students. At the beginning of the year, I have each student make silhouettes and I give them two hand cutouts and two close pins. I have them decorate the silhouettes so they resemble the student. I have the students glue the hand to the clothespins and then glue the clothespins to each side of the silhouette. Students hang their favorite work on the clothespin hands throughout the school year. Leave the silhouettes up all year and students enjoy decorating them with seasonal outfits or hats, as shown in the following photographs.

Photograph 4.1

In closing, the following poem is one I wrote from a series of entries of middle school pre-service teachers who reflected in a journal about their literacy experiences in the classroom. What I like about the poem is how it reflects the many different types of small challenges teachers face throughout the day, but how any day that ends in a smile makes all the problems disappear.

Today,
    was the worst day
    a challenge
    my time
    their work

I sat down,
    an open invitation
    talking
    doing
    teaching?

Tomorrow,
    introduce
    try
    their time
    be nice

Before they go,
    to see
    to think
    to tell
    to record

This experience,
    these kids
    don't listen
    finish my thoughts
    right answers

Today, the worst day,
  a voice
  a smile
  a kind word
Thank you, Mrs. *****

Teachers Thinking Deeply

Following is a list of questions and professional development resources that are recommended to teachers who want to reflect deeply
on their instructional practices in reading and writing.

Discussion Questions to Maintain and Extend Goal

What factors does your school face on a daily basis that impact your
thinking about literacy and your ability to demonstrate kindness?

1. What can you learn from your peers about procedures they follow
   that help minimize negative thoughts about students?

2. Exemplary teachers display kindness toward their students. What
   have you changed about your teaching instruction that allows
   students to feel that you respect them as a student?

Real-life Classroom Scenario

Jane is a fifth grader. She is essentially a nonreader. She can write a
few pre-primer words with some letter reversals. She is able to answer questions when the story is read to her. She has behavioral
mood swings. One minute she says she can't do something. The next
minute she states, "I'm not retarded, you teachers think I can't do
things. I can do some things myself." How would you respond?

Personal and Professional Literacy Resources

Following is a list of resources that I have used to become more knowledgeable in the area of teaching with kindness.

- Pressley, M., Dolezal, S. E., Raphael, L. M., Mohan, L., Roehrig, A. D., & Bogner, K. (2003). *Motivating primary-grade students.* New York: The Guilford Press. This book contains many motivational suggestions that can be integrated during reading and writing engagements.

- Block, C. C., & Israel, S. E. (2006). *Quotes to inspire great reading teachers.* Thousand   Oaks, CA: Corwin Press. Quotes are a great way to help students and teachers think deeply about their practice. Many of the quotes throughout this book provide recommendations for positive behaviors and actions for teachers to incorporate in the literacy classroom.

- Seabrook, J. (2004). *Furry logic: A guide to life's little challenges.* Berkeley, CA: Ten Speed Press. This is a fun book of lessons for teachers and students on how to treat others with kindness. This book can be used at the beginning of the day as a journal writing prompt or at the end of the day to reflect on lessons learned in school.

Goal #4: Understanding

Teacher Recognizes Assessment as Essential to Discovery of Self and Students

"I need to keep renewing my insight into my students' true condition in spite of misleading appearance. As I have come to understand my students' fears, I have been able to aim my teaching in a new direction. I no longer teach to their imputed ignorance, having rejected that assessment as both inaccurate and self-serving."

—Palmer, 1998, p. 46

Journaling Thoughts on Understanding

Why do you want to make a commitment to the learning behavior of understanding? Why will achieving this goal have an influence on instruction?

Thoughts for Group Discussion:

Self-Reflection: Making a Commitment

Goal Rationale:

Based on teaching standards from literacy organizations, assessment is important in the literacy development of students. Teachers who demonstrate that they value assessment exhibit behaviors that highlight their interest in understanding their students and self as a literacy teacher.

One of my co-teaching partners during my first years as a professor, used what is now one of my favorite children's literature books titled, *Thank you, Mr. Falker* by Polacco (1998) to model the importance of understanding students. She used the book at the start of class as a read-aloud. What I like about this story is Mr. Falker's determination in trying to understand how to help Tisha, a fifth grader who cannot read, learn to read. I think it takes determination, rather than frustration, when teachers are trying to understand students, especially ones who need more understanding than others do.

This chapter focuses on developing the literacy goal of understanding in two ways. First, this chapter will focus on using assessment as a tool to gain knowledge about students' literacy ability and beliefs about literacy. Second, this chapter will guide literacy educators understanding about self by using self-assessment and reflection as a tool to deeper understanding.

Understanding is the process or result of acquiring or constructing meaning (Harris & Hodges, 1995). From a philosophical perspective, understanding is the ability to see things differently, or to be aware of another's feelings (Svoboda, 2000). From an instructional perspective, understanding can be acquired when a teacher uses assessment as an essential tool to read inside the developing mind of a child to understand the student's academic and emotional strengths. Teachers can use assessment tools to reflect on philosophical and pedagogical beliefs.

I used the example above because everything we do can be a form of assessment. Pollaco is telling the story of Mr. Falker to explain that understanding Tisha was important to the success of his ability to teach her. Palmer's powerful quote about understanding our students and using assessment as a tool to learn about their fears has fueled his insight about students while guiding his teaching into new directions. My co-teacher also believed in the importance of understanding students and indirectly through her actions saw this characteristic as an important behavior.

Svoboda (2000) who is a teacher, philosopher, and anthropologist maintains the following, "The gift of understanding is sorely needed in a world such as ours, a world marked by excessive individualism, growing mistrust, accelerating violence and "isms" of all kind" (p. 97). Svoboda goes on to say that the opposite of understanding is a judgmental attitude. Being judgmental with our students and others is very easy. Judging ourselves and making a wise assessment is much more difficult. The ability to be understanding is something that I truly value as a teacher and educator. However, I also believe that the ability to possess the characteristic of understanding requires the mindset that in order to be exemplary in a profession, one needs to understand.

Of all the literacy goals that you are striving to attain, understanding is probably the most difficult to achieve. Everyone has probably said, "I do not understand." When you do understand, it feels like a revelation has taken place and it is exciting. Svoboda, so elegantly describes the difficulty of attaining the ability to understand when she writes:

> understanding is not easy to arrive at. In fact, it demands considerable asceticism—especially the asceticism of detachment and humility. Understanding demands detachment. It means, I must let go of my own way of looking at things—at least temporarily—in order to take up someone else's way of perceiving reality. (2000, p. 96)

To attain understanding related to a student's literacy ability, exemplary teachers recognize assessment as an essential part of daily instructional habits. The purpose of writing a chapter on the disposition of understanding is to help educators value assessments and to use the information to reflect on your practice.

What this chapter is not? When my book was going through peer review, one reviewer commented on the lack of assessments that were available in this chapter. The reviewer was looking for a chapter on assessment tools and reproducibles but that is not the purpose of this chapter or this book. With all due respect, this book is about reflecting on instructional behaviors that influence student learning, motivation, and professional development. This chapter is not about explaining the various types of assessments and providing you with more assessments on how to evaluate reading strategies. Several resources at the end of this chapter do an excellent job of highlighting assessment resources. Instead, the focus on this chapter is to help literacy educators reflect on their beliefs and behaviors of assessment utilization with the goal of using assessments as tools to understand students and self in order to change practice.

Current research on assessments supports one that allows teachers the opportunities to develop an understanding of their students' abilities in order to guide instruction. In order to develop a deeper understanding of the "self" as literacy educator and the "student" as a literacy learner, teachers are engaging in metacognitive forms of assessment. The practice of self-reflection and self-assessment is a form of metacognitive assessment. Metacognitive assessments are measures that evaluate the utilization of thinking processes and readers' thoughts related to or during literacy tasks and learning behaviors both cognitive and affective. Metacognitive assessments are valuable tools that aid teachers in identifying cognitive and affective capacity, as well as cognitive misunderstandings so that students can receive more effective and more appropriate literacy instruction (Israel et al., 2005).

Flavell (1979) encourages teachers to use metacognitive assessments as tools to discover literacy competencies for ensuing comprehension acquisition. This shift in thinking challenges teachers to develop a positive disposition about the purpose and value of assessments. In addition, require teachers to evaluate their pedagogical position on metacognitive-oriented instruction and focus more on developing the reader's strengths and look at inadequacies as goals for literacy improvement. Reflect on the negative factors that effect your disposition about assessments in order to identify effective assessment behaviors and behaviors that might require adjustments.

How do you view assessment in your classroom? What types of assessments do you find most valuable to helping you understand your students? Do you think observations are a form of assessment? Table 5.1 summarizes several negative factors that might prohibit you from understanding your students and your self as a literacy educator. Use this table to help you identify areas that you believe might deter you from being an understanding teacher.

Table 5.1   Factors That Minimize Teachers Ability to Understand Self and Students Checklist

_____	1. Teacher's own negative attitude about using assessments in the classroom.
_____	2. Not enough time to adequately administer and analyze assessments.
_____	3. Too many mandated assessments that overwhelm students and teachers.
_____	4. Inadequate assessment resources for teachers to effectively, obtain practical data on a student's reading and writing ability.

(Continued on next page)

**Table 5.1   Factors That Minimize Teachers Ability to Understand
Self and Students Checklist** *(Continued)*

_____   5. False information reported by previous teachers or missing information in files on at-risk students.

_____   6. Lack of funding available for assessments.

_____   7. Negative public policy on assessment utilization related to standardized test taking.

_____   8. Parental concerns about assessment reporting in the larger school community.

_____   9. Colleagues who do not place the same level of importance on assessments and therefore do not value time spent on assessment administration decreasing the amount of data available to help students' performance and achievement.

_____   10. Teacher's belief that he or she is already an exemplary teacher and therefore does not want to take time to reflect on practice.

_____   11. Other negative factors

 Review the list and reflect on the factors you have checked. Do you notice any trends with your responses? Are their other factors that need to be considered?

_____

_____

_____

_____

_____

_____

_____

_____

_____

_____

_____

_____

_____

_____

Observation from a Window into Literacy Lives

Recently my daughter came home from school and painted her science board for the science fair. The next day the board had rolled up from the wet paint. I suggested she try to flatten the board. She said she was not going to do that because her board stands out from all the others and when I go to locate my board after the teacher grades it, it will be easier for me to find it in the stack. I asked her what she meant by her board standing out. She said, all that matters is how her board looks and how her binder of research matches her board. The teachers only look at the board anyway so it is not going to matter how crappy my project is. That is why I am putting all my effort into my board. Therefore, I concluded with her in agreement that the only thing that matters is the board. She said, exactly!

Consider how your students might feel about how you assess their work. How would they explain to their parents what is most important to you about grading and assignments?

Self-questioning to Achieve Goal

Self-questioning to Achieve Goal

What challenges do you experience that keep you from being understanding?

How Colleagues Overcome Challenges:

What did you learn about your beliefs on assessments from the checklist above? Do you believe that assessments will enable teachers to understand students and self in a way that will provide evidence for change or improvement in literacy achievement? What behaviors do you currently display that demonstrate how you understand your students? Following are three challenges that impact assessment outcomes and suggestions for how teachers can overcome them.

Assessments Present Their Own Levels of Difficulty

Assessment is a part of the classroom culture. Teachers often are faced with having to spend additional time explaining assessments prior to administration of the assessment. Teachers can alleviate some of the students' fears about taking assessments by making sure instructions to students are consistent and clear. Teachers can direct students how to solve a problem when taking assessments, teachers can say, "When something is unclear stop and reread the sentence or the directions to make sure you understand what is being asked of you." Teachers should also use appropriate language when giving directions.

Some students struggle with taking assessments because they are unclear about what is being asked of them or they do not have the ability to read and understand some of the terms within the assessment directions. Spending time explaining assessment terminology will help eliminate student fears about assessments. In addition, it is helpful for students to understand the rationale for taking the assessment and how this assessment will be used in the future. Some tips for assessment administration that I have used over the years are as follows:

- Explain in advance what the assessment will be used for and how the assessments will be scored.

- Provide immediate feedback for the students. I provide students with the answer sheets and allow them to grade their own papers. I always check all the papers, but students feel good about leaving class knowing how they have done on an exam.

- Provide students with an overhead or visual aid of sample test questions or items they will experience on the test. Many students have anxiety about exams or assessments because they do not know how to study or what to expect. Table 5.2 can be used to help teachers understand what students are thinking about assessments in the classroom and the teacher's demonstration of how well they understand their students.

Table 5.2   Teacher Understanding Inventory

Directions: Respond to the following question. Provide as much detail as you can when responding. You may have an adult help you record your answers if necessary.

1. Do you feel comfortable with taking assessments?

2. Give an example of when I showed how assessments helped me to understanding your abilities. Why do you remember this?

3. Do you recall a time when you think I did not understand your ability? What should I have done differently?

4. Do you have any other suggestions or comments on assessments?

Assessments Do Not Allow Teachers to Think Differently about Literacy

Two types of research-based metacognitive assessments teachers will find useful are interviews, and surveys or inventories. Different assessments can be used to obtain different types of information. I like to use the following assessments with my students.

Interviews.   During the first week of school, I like to conduct one-on-one interviews with my students to learn about their reading and writing preferences. I usually ask them questions as follows:

1. What do you like about reading and writing?
2. What types of books do you prefer to read?
3. If you could write about something, what would you like to write about?

Inventories.   Another easy assessment I like to use early in the school year or semester is something I call a "Fears Inventory." This inventory asks students to identify their fears about a topic or fears about what they will be doing in reading and writing. Table 5.3 is an example of a "Fears Inventory" I use with my older students.

Table 5.3   Sample Fears Inventory on Literacy

Explain your *fears* about taking this class, or *fears* you have about reading.

Explain your *fears* about writing.

How can I help you overcome your *fear*?

Assessments Increase Student Anxiety

When teachers say anything about testing or assessment, it is safe to assume that the anxiety levels of students will increase because of that. Develop a teacher sense of test anxiety and incorporate behaviors to help reduce that anxiety prior to test taking. One way to reduce testing anxiety is by building confidence. I believe that if students do not feel confident prior to taking an examination, then they have not adequately learned the material or have had so many negative experiences with testing they have developed a lack of confidence about testing, which might influence their achievement. Prior to any assessment, I like to make sure students understand three things:

1. The purpose of the test
2. The testing format and length
3. How the testing results will be used; to change instruction, to identify strengths, and so forth

One reviewer recommended using a Cognitive Coaching strategy. The reviewer explains as follows:

I was reminded of an activity I heard of in a Cognitive Coach training. The facilitator showed us a "move" to help students before they took a test. She had them move around the room in an organized way to talk about what in their opinions were the important things to re-member before the test, quiz, or assessment they were about to take. Teachers can use this same activity to allow students to ask questions or explain something they need to know.

Teachers can maximize testing results by reducing test anxiety. A wonderful story to read to students at the beginning of the school year or prior to a test is *Testing Miss. Malarkey* by Judy Finchler (2000). Another way to reduce test anxiety is to place three columns on the chalkboard like this:

Information I am confident I know...	Information I think I know...	Information I need clarification on...

Invite all or half the students to go to the board and begin completing the large visual assessment. Students can work in any columns and move between columns or they can work in pairs with one person responsible for writing down information. Teachers will be able to identify areas students are confident about or need clarification on prior to the test.

Challenges in my classroom that negatively influence my ability to understand my students and my self as a literacy teacher are:

_____

_____

_____

_____

_____

_____

_____

_____

_____

_____

_____

_____

_____

_____

_____

_____

_____

Strategies on how to overcome challenges and increase my level of understanding are:

_____

_____

_____

_____

_____

_____

_____

_____

_____

_____

_____

_____

_____

_____

_____

_____

_____

Self-evaluation of Progress

Self-evaluation of Progress

Have you achieved your goal? If not, what positive action can you take to achieve the goal?

New Ideas:

This chapter has helped you identify your level of understanding of your students and your teaching abilities in order to help you realize the literacy goal of understanding. The goals of this chapter were as follows:

- Use assessments to understand your students and benefits of the literacy curriculum
- Apply the principles of assessments in order to reach the literacy goal of understanding
- Understand the principles of how to use metacognitive assessments in your classroom to obtain cognitive and affective knowledge about your students and about you as a literacy educator

- Learn about key aspects of the different types of literacy assessments
- Develop a positive attitude about assessment and view assessment as an effective tool to gain understanding with self and students
- Learn how to develop your own literacy assessments to fit your teaching needs

 My personal literacy goal to become understanding of my students and recognize assessment as essential is:

_____

_____

_____

_____

_____

_____

_____

_____

_____

_____

_____

_____

_____

The reason this goal is important to me is:

_____

_____

_____

_____

_____

_____

_____

_____

_____

_____

_____

_____

Prior to the conclusion of this chapter is a Self-monitoring checklist to help you evaluate how you value assessment as a tool to better understand self and students.

Self-monitoring Checklist

Self-monitoring Statement	Behaviors you Display	Actions to Take to Show Enthusiasm
How do you demonstrate that you view assessment as essential to self and students?		
What are your beliefs about assessment and how do your attitudes affect your beliefs?		
Do you find it difficult to view assessments as a valuable tool to increase student literacy achievement?		
What literacy assessments do you find difficult or challenging to administer?		
Do you have a wide variety of assessment tools to meet the needs of all learners?		
How do you differentiate assessments in order to improve student learning and your own level of understanding?		
How do you overcome your inability to understand certain students with learning difficulties?		
What do your students believe about assessments in the culture of your classroom?		
What kind of assessments do you use in order to understand your teaching abilities with the goal of improving instruction?		

Teaching Ideas for the Literacy Classroom

My Thoughts on Teaching Understanding

How will you help your students develop behaviors of understanding?

How will you invite students to set individual goals?

To achieve the goal of understanding self and students consider implementing some of the following ideas when using assessments.

Robust Reflections

To help increase metacognitive thinking with your students so they can communicate thoughts to you more fully, use "meta-books" where characters come to life and talk to the reader. A few of my favorite meta-picture books are listed in Table 5.4. The following books can also be used to develop writing prompts for journaling. Read the books and invite students to think of writing prompts for journaling.

Teachers can use the prompts to understand students deeper thinking about literacy ability.

Table 5.4   Metacognitive Picture Books That Bring Characters to Life

Galileo's Treasure Box by Catherine Brighton (1987). Published by Walker & Company, New York.

Diary of a Worm by Doreen Cronin (2003) Published by Harper Collins, New York.

You Read to Me, I'll Read to You by Mary Ann Hoberman (2004). Published by Scholastic, New York.

Plantzilla Goes to Camp by Jerdine Nolen (2006). Published by Simon & Schuster, New York.

The Story of the Search for the Story by Bjern Sortland (2000). Published by Carolrhoda Books, Inc., Minneapolis, MN.

Detective LaRue: Letters from the Investigation by Mark Teague (2004). Published by Scholastic Press, New York.

Assessing Assessments

One of the biggest issues I hear from both pre-service and in-service teachers is the issue of time. Over the years, teachers have let me know that assessments are very time consuming. In addition, teachers tend to think there are just too many assessments floating around and they are either assessing too much or so frustrated about which assessments to use that they don't know where to begin. I addressed this issue, which was the same one for me when I was teaching, by periodically performing an assessment evaluation. Table 5.5 summarizes an Assessment Inventory format that you can follow to evaluate and critique the type of assessments you are currently using and why. Teachers have found this inventory to be particularly helpful in identifying specific assessments they may no longer need to use, which frees up time or new assessments they would like to implement.

Table 5.5   Assessment Inventory Tool

Pre-Inventory Reflection Questions:

- What assessments are you currently using to evaluate literacy?
- How do your colleagues use assessments?
- Are assessments school or district mandated?
- Why do you use these assessments?
- Do you analyze your assessments?
- How do you use your assessments to inform instruction?
- How do your students feel about assessments?
- What have you learned in the past about your teaching from data on assessments you have used?

Assessment Component	Description	Evaluation Guidelines
Assessments Being Used	Gather and review the literacy assessments you are currently using in your class and make a list.	What are the goals for each of the assessments? Explain how you use the assessments. How do you see the assessments you are currently using related to your overall philosophy of literacy and assessment? Describe the strengths and weaknesses of the assessments?
Deleted Assessments	List the assessments or procedures you need to remove.	What is your rationale for deleting the assessments from your classroom?
New Assessments to Implement	List of new assessments you want to add.	Explain your rationale for the new assessments. What would you like to gain from using the new assessments?
Instructional Change	Based on the assessments you will now use, describe interventions or instructional changes you will integrate.	Based on the assessments you are currently using, how will they inform instruction? How will they help you understand self and students? What are your goals based on the new assessments?

(Continued on next page)

Table 5.5   Assessment Inventory Tool *(Continued)*

Sample Assessment Inventory (5th grade Teacher)

Assessment Component	Summary	Evaluation Reflections
Assessments Being Used	DIBELS, DRA, Journals, Ongoing Work, Site Words, Conferences District Created Assessments	DRA is used to make informed decisions about reading and help guide weekly conference discussions with students. Assessment date from ongoing work, site words, and journals are used to form literacy groups, guide mini-lessons, and inform students of progress on weekly reports.
Deleted Assessments	DRA	The DRA is very time consuming and I am not sure if there is an efficient way to begin testing students on the right level. I do not have an adequate comprehension assessment.
New Assessments to Implement	QRI-IV	The QRI-IV would give me more flexibility is looking at students' comprehension abilities. The QRI-IV is a lot easier to administer.
Instructional Change	Become familiar with more technology-related assessment tools.	I need to learn more about how to use technology as an assessment tool and use more Internet resources that can help me save time.

eAssessment Tools

Because so many teachers are concerned about the amount of time it takes to assess students, I have compiled a list of assessments that teachers can use to help them use their time wisely. The list of eAssessment Tools are summarized in Table 5.6.

Table 5.6   Summary of eAssessment Time Saving Tools for Literacy Teachers

eAssessment	Description
www.mitest.com	Test of Multiple Intelligence. Easy to use. Students receive a printed report summarizing their intelligence strengths.
www.leapfrogstore.com	Leap Frog Work Stations. Can be purchased on local Target stores or teacher supply stores. Helps students with all aspects of literacy including phonics.
www.phonicsdance.com	The Phonics Dance: A Six Step to Literacy in the Primary Grades dance program that focuses on word attack skills and basic phonics memorization through songs and dance.
www.homeclubs.scholastic.com	A program to help beginning readers at home. The cost is minimal and parents and teachers will love using this program.
www.stepuptowriting.com	A writing program that helps students identify writing strengths and areas for improvement.
www.engine-uity.com	Engine-Uity is a program that allows teachers to create assessments, as well as learning center tools and activities.
www.nwrel.org	Online classroom assessment resources for teachers in elementary and secondary grades who want to learn more about how assessments can help teachers understand students.
www.learning-styles-online.com	Free learning styles inventory and graphical results that provides a guide to personal learning styles.
www.iste.org	Microsoft will make available an online assessment tool of technology literacy in Middle Schoolers that can be obtained from the International Society for Technology.

After reading this chapter, you are working toward achieving four goals thus far. Enthusiasm in the classroom will help motivate your students to want to read. Unity builds community. Kindness nurtures a positive literacy environment. Finally, understanding informs your practice and moves you closer to becoming an exemplary literacy teacher. A famous quote by Louis L' Amour that helps position teaching behaviors of understanding within reading and writing education is, "Education should equip a person to live life well, to understand what is happening about him, for to live life well one must live with awareness" (Quote from Block & Israel, 2006)

Teachers Thinking Deeply

Following is a list of questions and professional development resources that are recommended to teachers who want to reflect deeply on their literacy practices.

Discussion Questions to Maintain and Extend Goal

1. After reading this chapter, what connections can you make with other esteemed literacy educators who seek to find understanding of their practice and of their students in order to improve your own literacy instruction?

2. Reflect on the demands of you as an educator in terms of assessment expectations. In your own teaching situation, how does using assessments allow you to understand your students more fully? What changes in your behaviors can you make in order to increase effectiveness of assessment utilization?

3. Exemplary teachers display understanding of their students relative to cognitive and affective abilities. What assessments do you use to provide you with measures that permit you to understand your students?

4. What assessments would you like to administer but for which you need more explanation on administration and analysis procedures? How will you obtain this information? What peers do you know who do a good job of using assessment as a tool to understand students? What type of assessments do they use?

5. Hold a discussion with your peers on what it means to understand your teaching and your students. What practices do your colleagues integrate in literacy to understand their students? What assessments do they find practical as well as informative? What assessments do not help understand students' literacy abilities?

Real-life Classroom Scenario

Mark is a 13-year-old boy entering middle school. He has Down syndrome and performs on a 1st and 2nd grade level. He struggles with math writing. He does not like to write because he says it takes him to long to scribe his answers. Mark refuses to write down anything in school. He is unorganized because he won't use a planner; thus he misses many assignments. He does not seem to be making any progress in his grades because he doesn't write down his homework or turn anything in to his teacher. What can you use that Mark has done in the past to help him focus on strengths to increase his writing ability? Are there any homework assignments you can evaluate to review Mark's progress? How would you evaluate those assignments? What would you look for?

Personal and Professional Literacy Resources

- Zull, J. E. (2002). *The Art of Changing the Brain.* Sterling, VA: Stylus Publishing. This book will help teachers think differently about how the brain processes information and how knowing this information can guide literacy instruction.
- Block, C. C., & Mangieri, J. N. (2003). *Exemplary Literacy Teachers: Promoting Success for All Children in Grades K-5.* New York: Guilford Press. This book will help teachers understand themselves as a teacher and what attributes they possess as a successful classroom teacher. The book contains a helpful teacher self-assessment that identifies teaching strengths and can be used by all teachers and educators who work with children in the primary grades.
- Barrentine, S. J., & Stokes, S. M. (2005). (Eds). *Reading Assessment: Principles and Practices for Elementary Teachers (2nd ed.).* Newark, DE: The International Reading Association. Teachers who want to learn about the different assessments related to reading and writing that can be used with all students will find this book extremely valuable when administering both informal and formal assessments.

Goal #5: Pursuit of Knowledge

Teacher Is Passionate About Professional Development

"Change that emanates from teachers lasts until they find a better way."

—Roland Bart, Improving Schools From Within
(Quote source: www.teachermentors.com)

Professional development has always been something very important to me. As a fourth grade teacher, I was always looking for a better way to teach literacy. I wanted my students to leave school every day feeling as though the time spent in my classroom was beneficial to them and the books that we shared during the day would become topics of conversation with their parents or friends in the evening. In addition, I also wanted them to leave my class with a sense of anticipation for the next day.

In order for me to achieve that goal, I valued opportunities to gain knowledge and was always seeking knowledge to make my classroom a better place for my students. I sought resources that were the landmark studies in my areas of interest at the time, such as reading comprehension. I would call publishers and request a list of their best-selling literacy resources in order to purchase ones that other exemplary teachers might be reading. I took advantage of professional organizations such as the International Reading Association by reading the journals and participating in service-related opportunities. I also volunteered for leadership roles at my school so as to engage in thoughtful discussions about literacy curriculum with my peers.

Journaling Thoughts on Knowledge

Why do you want to make a commitment to the learning behavior of knowledge? Why will achieving this goal have an influence on instruction?

Thoughts for Group Discussion:

Self-Reflection: Making a Commitment

Goal Rationale:

National literacy organizations set high standards for teachers regarding professional development. Through professional development, teachers exhibit behaviors that demonstrate they value reflection and commitment to personal growth as a necessity to exemplary instruction.

How will you use research and professional development opportunities to enhance literacy instruction? How can professional development influence teaching? When I reflect on professional development and the impact I think learning has on my students and the larger school community, I think about how my students will benefit from my knowledge gained through professional development opportunities. Results of professional development are difficult to measure; however, literacy growth and achievement of students are reliable indicators.

This chapter focuses on helping you come closer to achieving the literacy goal of knowledge. To acquire knowledge a teacher must possess the desire to learn and develop a greater appreciation and passion for professional development.

Two major initiatives have shaped how we view professional development in literacy instruction: *No Child Left Behind* and *The Report of the National Reading Panel* (2000). *The Report of the National Reading Panel* (2000), which is reforming how we teach reading, related that "in-service professional development does lead to improved teacher knowledge and practice and student achievement" (5–12). In order to be effective, professional development at the in-service level needs extensive support in money and time. Regarding effectiveness, one aspect that can be taught and that influenced professional development was "teacher attitude." The report states, "This is an important finding because it is the predisposition of teachers to change that makes change possible. Without a change in attitude, it is extremely difficult to effect changes in practice" (5–14). What teachers can learn from the report of The National Reading Panel is:

- Professional development is a valuable component of exemplary literacy instruction
- Knowledge is a predisposition to effective practice
- An important outcome of professional development is improvement in student achievement

Without student achievement, the literacy deficit will not improve. Therefore, it makes sense for teachers, at all levels, to welcome and be engaged in ongoing professional development opportunities. Most teachers do realize this and it shows through their enthusiasm for learning outside the classroom in order to improve instruction as well as their personal growth as a teacher. How can educators develop professional development opportunities that are more engaging and related to specific needs of teachers? How can educators motivate teachers to appreciate the value of professional development? How can we encourage more teachers to join professional development organizations? How can universities develop more opportunities to help teachers share their knowledge at professional conferences in their area of interest, such as the International Reading Association?

Pressley (2006) found in a study of effective "whole schools and classrooms" that the most effective teachers were passionate about professional development and had a greater openness to improvement. Similar to the findings of *The National Reading Panel,* in that, openness to improvement is based on teacher attitude regarding willingness to change, the most effective schools were ones in which all the teachers and administration valued professional development. He reports:

> Let me tell you about one of the most consistent in our interviews of teachers over the years. It is always the most effective teachers who have told us that they have much more to learn. They are always the ones seeking the professional development. The weaker teachers are often very confident that they already teach well."
> (Pressley, 2006, p. 6)

Pressley describes effective schools as "academically focused." Pressley (2006) has strong recommendations for the future about how teachers respond to professional development and that is to select teachers with the attitude that they need to get better and for schools to seek ways to help them do so. Pressley also recommends that for the teachers who lack talent and a willingness to engage in professional development opportunities, that they be counseled out of teaching. Since professional development is expensive, those who want and desire professional development should receive it, and be encouraged to stay in the profession.

Reflection on your beliefs about the literacy goal of knowledge and your level of passion for professional development can help you learn more about your attitudes and willingness to change. This book also supports their suggestion, with the major goal of this chapter being to help you understand your beliefs about professional development. Table 6.1 will help you reflect on what factors might contribute to any negative beliefs you might have about professional development.

Table 6.1   Factors that Decrease Motivation for Engaging in Professional Development Checklist

_____ 1. Teachers own negative attitude about professional development.

_____ 2. Professional development is too time consuming for busy class-room teachers.

_____ 3. The professional development available is too expensive.

_____ 4. Funds are being spent on building renovations or curriculum materials rather than ways for teachers to learn more about their profession.

_____ 5. Professional organizations are too expensive to join.

_____ 6. Mandatory professional development workshops do not meet teacher's needs.

_____ 7. Teacher feels adequate with current level of education and has no desire to continue taking educational courses.

_____ 8. Factors such as personal constraints and family commitments get in the way of professional development opportunities.

_____ 9. Administration does not value professional development.

_____ 10. Growth in terms of reflective evaluation of self is difficult.

_____ 11. Other Factors

Review the list and reflect on the factors you have checked. Do you notice any trends with your responses? Are their other factors that need to be considered?

_____

_____

_____

_____

_____

_____

_____

_____

_____

_____

Observation from a Window into Literacy Lives

When I was a classroom teacher, our school was going through the annual accreditation process. I was asked to lead the group on professional development. I thought this was so exciting until we started meeting. Prior to our meetings, I did a lot of research on professional development with teachers. I created packets that participants in our group could read. The first problem I faced with my group was a lack of attendance by group members. The third problem I had was parents who were committed to high teaching standards regarding professional development for all teachers and being very loud about their beliefs with other parents and teachers. I learned from the parents that they want their child to have teachers that hold masters degrees or higher because they believe teachers with advanced degrees are better teachers. I learned from the teachers that you could not force professional development on them, they have to desire it. In the end, our committee decided to propose a professional development library for teachers where they could go and read books they want to read, as well as to engage in study groups with peers they liked to be with.

Consider how you might have felt being the committee leader on a professional development committee where members had different beliefs about professional development. Have you been in similar situations? How would you handle this situation differently?

Self-questioning to Achieve Goal

Self-questioning to Achieve Goal

What challenges do you experience that keep you from pursuing knowledge to increase professional development?

How Colleagues Overcome Challenges:

How do you feel about professional development opportunities? What aspects of literacy would you like to learn more about? Do you have access to affordable professional development opportunities that you will benefit from? Following are three factors that might negatively influence your ability to value professional development.

Creative Ways to Obtain Professional Resources

One factor that may discourage you from engaging in growing professionally is your lack of knowledge about resources available that might positively address your literacy situation. In addition, you might not be aware of some of the new books or resources available since research is always changing. Learning more about effective professional development resources is to seek advice from exceptional teachers around the country in your field. When you attend conferences, get to know other teachers in similar teaching situations as your own. Teachers can also find professional development opportunities from leading publishers in literacy and teacher education.

Suggest Professional Development Alternatives

Most in-service programs are directed to whole-school improvement plans. This may not be as effective as it could be since not all teachers need exactly the same type of professional development. Like students, teachers need choices. One strategy you can use to get the most out of your professional development programs is to suggest alternatives that suit your needs. Make a list of professional development goals and try to do some advance research on other opportunities. Like students, teachers need choices as well. Perhaps you could offer to plan an alternative session during in-service programs. You might also suggest voluntary professional development programs (Allen, 2006; Pressley, 2006). By offering teachers a choice about professional development opportunities, they are motivated to actively participate during learning engagements.

Model Positive Behavior about Professional Development

If you have a negative attitude about professional development or you have experienced professional development programs from which you have not gained any knowledge from, then try to think differently about your approach to professional development. You have heard the cliché "think outside the box." What does thinking differently about your approach to professional development mean to you? Many districts and schools pre-plan professional development opportunities in advance and these programs usually are driven based on state or local reform initiatives. Novice and beginning teachers, through proficient ones, can use a different approach to planning their personal professional development programs.

If you were to think differently about professional development, or think outside the box, you might reflect the perspective of your students and their academic achievement goals. One of the ways I go about planning professional development for myself is asking myself a question, "what is it the students in my class this year need to help them be successful?"

At the beginning of my classes, one of my priorities is getting to know my students. I have attached an assessment that I use on the first day of class. If you are in a teaching situation where you have large classes, I suggest you have each student complete one, then put them in smaller groups and complete the same form together using the data from individual assessments but call it a group profile. This will help you only look at four "class profiles" trends by class. Have each group put all the student inquiry surveys with the one-group survey so you can look at the individual student surveys when you have time.

If you are a primary class teacher, you can modify the questions and send the form home for parents to fill out with their child. Students can bring the completed form on the first day of school. Table 6.2a is the assessment I created to help me get to know my undergraduate students. Table 6.2b is a modified version for primary grade teachers. I used something similar as a classroom teacher. This assessment is valuable for any teachers and can be adapted as needed. One way to make adaptations for special needs students is to have them select the questions that are most important or only answer half the questions depending on time.

Table 6.2a Student Inquiry Survey

Name: Date: E-mail:	
The purpose of this survey is to find out as much as I can about you in order to help you learn. Please respond to each of the questions as best as you can. The questions will help you with deeper and more critical thinking as it relates to your course goals and expectations, as well as provide insight about your learning pathways. Use other side if you need more space. Thank you, Dr. Israel	
1. Describe your current ambitions.	
2. What are your approaches to and conceptions of learning?	
3. What are your approaches to reading difficult text? What are your struggles?	

(Continued on next page)

Table 6.2a   Student Inquiry Survey *(Continued)*

---

4. Explain how you reason.

5. What is your temperament? What is your teaching temperament?

6. What are your habits of the heart and mind?

7. What daily matters occupy your attention?

8. What five senses do you identify with most and why?

9. What is your hypothesis about how students learn to read?

10. What conclusions do you hope to draw by the end of this course?

(Bain, K. (2004). What the best college teachers do. Cambridge, MA: Harvard University Press)

Table 6.2b   Primary-Grade Student Inquiry Survey

Name: Date:

The purpose of this survey is to find out as much as I can about you in order to help you learn. Please respond to each of the questions as best as you can. The questions will help you with deeper and more critical thinking as it relates to your course goals and expectations, as well as provide insight about your learning pathways. Use other side if you need more space.

1. Describe your dream.

2. What helps you learn best?

3. What do you do when you have trouble reading?

4. Tell me how you might solve a problem.

5. Describe your personality.

6. What occupies your attention?

7. What five senses do you identify with most and why?

8. What do you love most?

Challenges in my classroom that negatively influence my ability to appreciate and value professional development in the area of reading and writing are:

_____

_____

_____

_____

_____

_____

_____

_____

_____

_____

_____

_____

_____

_____

_____

_____

_____

Strategies on how to overcome challenges and increase my level of knowledge are:

_____

_____

_____

_____

_____

_____

_____

_____

_____

_____

_____

_____

_____

_____

_____

_____

_____

_____

Self-evaluation of Progress

Self-evaluation of Progress

Have you achieved your goal? If not, what positive action can you take to achieve the goal?

New Ideas:

In this chapter, you have learned more about your beliefs about professional development in order to reach the literacy goal of knowledge. You obtained some specific strategies to be more passionate about professional development in order to improve your knowledge about literacy instruction. You have also addressed some possible negative attitudes about why you may not value professional development opportunities. How close are you to achieving your goals? The goals of this chapter that you have realized are:

- Evaluate your disposition about professional development and make decisions about areas in which you would like to grow professionally

- Critically reflect on your level of professional development in terms of stages of your performance
- Understand the importance of professional development as a literacy educator
- Use knowledge as a tool to motivate learning and enhance literacy instruction

As a teacher, it is normal to feel as though time spent learning might not benefit students. The evidence of how professional development might have influenced my literacy instruction is written in the cards and notes that I received on the last day of my teaching career. Table 6.3 provides a sample assessment teachers can use with students or parents to learn more about their perceptions regarding your level of knowledge. Below are three lessons I learned from my students and parents about the value of professional development through the lens of recorded comments from my cards and notes.

Choose topics to study that yield results for the larger school community

I studied parental involvement and tried to find ways to use all my parents in my classroom. One parent wrote, "Working with you, in fourth grade, was the beginning of my classroom involvement." Reflecting on this note helped me realize that parents value teachers who engage in seeking professional development opportunities as well as teachers who are knowledgeable about pedagogy and content areas.

Learn more about your topics of passion

I have always been passionate about helping my students make connections with what they are reading in order to increase reading comprehension. There are several experiences that have helped me desire to learn more about effective comprehension strategies. First, I have always been an excellent reader; however, I have struggled with reading comprehension and this has always bothered me. I never understood how it was possible that I could be such a good reader but score poorly on reading comprehension. What also changed the way I think about learning more about effective reading comprehension strategies is when a parent of a gifted child wanted to know whether her son could not comprehend text. Because I was unable to respond to this question, I decided to do more research in the area of reading comprehension.

One of the aspects I studied related to reading comprehension was the influence of creativity to enhance learning. I learned how important it was to find ways to use research to connect with the students. One girl in my class wrote, "I had so much fun going on field trips, doing speeches, book reports, and creative writing. I really liked the creative ideas." This made me realize that my students were valuing what I was learning about outside of class.

Learn about issues valued by the school and community

When this observation note was written, cooperative learning groups were part of our professional development goals. I also was interested in drama to enhance reading comprehension, so I used my knowledge of cooperative learning groups and integrated the methodology with plays. I found that cooperative learning groups were a motivator, as well as a way to enhance reading skills. My principal wrote a note stating, "Today, I enjoyed the team approach you used to help the kids develop their play. You are doing much of what was recommended at Friday's workshop. The students took their jobs seriously. You took the role of coach and really helped provide direction for the kids."

Table 6.3   Teacher Knowledge Inventory

Directions: Respond to the following question. Provide as much detail as you can when responding. You may have an adult help you record your answers if necessary.

1. How does your teacher demonstrate knowledge of literacy?

2. Give an example of when your teacher tried something new and you learned from it?

3. Do you think your teacher is knowledgeable about subject matter?

4. Do you have any other suggestions you can share on the "knowledge" of literacy and instruction related to your teacher?

My personal literacy goal to grow in knowledge by becoming passionate about professional development is:

_____

_____

_____

_____

_____

_____

_____

_____

_____

_____

_____

_____

_____

_____

The reason this goal is important to me is:

_____

_____

_____

_____

_____

_____

_____

_____

_____

_____

_____

_____

_____

_____

Think about the personal goals you have set for yourself regarding your level of passion for professional development and how you demonstrate that you are passionate about knowledge. Evaluate your progress by using the following checklist to see if you have come closer to your goal.

Self-monitoring Checklist

Self-monitoring Statement	Behaviors you Display	Actions to Consider
What do you do to show you value professional development?		
What do you gain from professional organizations?		
What areas of literacy are you passionate about?		
After you attend a professional development session, how do you act?		
When someone invites you to lead a research group or study group, what would you do?		

Teaching Ideas for the Literacy Classroom

My Thoughts on Teaching Enthusiasm

Now you want to help your students be more enthusiastic about reading and writing. What can you do to help them achieve this goal?

How will you invite students to set individual goals to achieve Enthusiasm in Reading and Writing:

Exemplary teachers engage in professional development and value knowledge as a way to influence practice. To help integrate the goal of knowledge in a literacy classroom, use some of the following teaching ideas.

Professional Development for the Soul

Teachers are very busy and professional development can be time consuming. Some very simple ways to start increasing professional development but not spend a huge amount of money or time is to try joining a research study group on a topic of interest. Many research study groups engage in online communication about the research sending emails periodically to suggest ideas or seek information on the topic. One of my favorite sources to join a research study group is from my membership with the National Reading Conference (NRC). Members are invited to join a listserve. I have learned so much about research and have so many opportunities come my way through this listserve that I think I would be lost in my profession without it. Here is where you can go to join NRC www.nrconline.org

eProfessional Development Opportunities

Subscribe to online literacy journals that send period reviews of research. I recommend you start with the International Reading Association at www.reading.org. I am also a member of National Council Teachers of English www.ncte.org where I receive periodic updates on literacy issues. I also subscribe to the online version of *Education Weekly* www.educationweekly.org. More recently, I became a member of *Publishers Weekly* where I receive daily updates and reviews about children's literature. I love this online resource. You can go to www.publishersweekly.org to join.

Professional Development Needs Assessments

Consider using a professional development needs assessment prior to planning your professional development. If you are a classroom teacher, use the needs assessment to encourage administration to provide choices during in-service programs or work with other schools to share resources. If you are a school administrator or literacy coach responsible for planning professional development workshops, use a needs assessment to obtain information about what teachers need in order to guide instruction. Table 6.4 provides an example of a Needs Assessment you can use.

Table 6.4   Needs Assessment for Professional Development

1. What professional development opportunities have been especially powerful for you and why?

2. What do you feel is your greatest area of need in the classroom and something you need to learn more about?

3. What are the strengths of the professional development opportunities available for you in school?

4. What are the weaknesses of the professional development opportunities available for you?

5. What are your personal goals regarding professional development?

6. Other comments or suggestions.

I started using a similar Professional Development needs assessment when doing in-service workshops for schools in order to address the actual literacy needs of the teachers. My rationale for using a needs assessment was that I have been the victim of boring professional development lectures and I did not want my audience to be bored when I gave a presentation. After having each of the teachers in the school complete the needs assessment, I created a list of responses that I used to guide my presentation. The results of the assessments are summarized in Table 6.5 along with the agenda that I used to guide my presentation. After the in-service, I received many accolades from the teachers saying they thought the information presented was particularly valuable to them. I was glad to hear they were not bored.

Table 6.5   Summary of School X Needs Assessment and Presentation Agenda

Assessment Item	Primary Teacher Needs	Middle School Teacher Needs	Special Area Teacher Needs
1. Prior PD valued	-enjoyed hands-on sessions -liked hearing how to implement Writing Traits	-learned about writing research topics -shared issues of concern and learned how peers were responding	-collaborated with classroom teachers on new writing ideas
2. Greatest PD need	-Need to know how to assess writing strengths -Need to know how to help students review work	-Need to learn how to evaluate research papers -Need journal writing ideas	-Would like to learn what the classroom teachers are doing so we can be included
3. PD Strengths	Ability to share ideas	Ability to share ideas	Ability to learn from peers
4. PD Weaknesses	Too much scattered information at once with no real stuff to use in the classroom	Information is geared to primary grade teachers only	No ideas on how to integrate writing with special area teachers
5. Goals/ Comments	Practical ideas on writing with primary students	Integrating writing standards across content areas	Working with classroom teachers and more time for classroom teachers to work with us.

Presentation Agenda

1. Introduction/Overview of Presentation Goals
2. Review of Needs Assessment
3. Group Journal Writing Activity: List five writing prompts that you can use in your classroom. (Prompts were gathered and placed in a School Writing Prompts Book that teachers took back with them that same day)
4. Review of Research on Writing
5. Small Break out Groups by Grade Levels—Special Areas Teachers Choose Group to work with: Goal to generate new writing unit together and share past ideas
6. Return to large group and share ideas
7. Review and Set Future Goals
8. Closing Comments From Teachers About Something Learned

Knowledge is something that you will have for a lifetime, but knowledge is always changing. Knowledge helps you get closer to wisdom. Knowing that student achievement is an outcome of professional development, teachers should be open to professional development opportunities. Reflecting on your disposition related to your level of passion about professional development will guide your professional development behaviors and help you find opportunities that fit your needs.

Teachers Thinking Deeply

Following is a list of questions and professional development resources that are recommended to teachers who want to reflect deeply on their instructional practices in reading and writing.

Discussion Questions to Maintain and Extend Goal

1. How would you evaluate your school's level of professional development opportunities?
2. What suggestions can you make to your school administration on how professional development can be enhanced?
3. How does knowledge influence pedagogy?
4. Do you believe parents value teachers who are knowledgeable about teaching and content?
5. What have your colleagues learned from attendance at professional development seminars this year?
6. What would you like the literacy coach or reading specialist in your school help you with in the area of reading and writing?

Real-life Classroom Scenario

I observe in a pre-school classroom and there is a little boy who does not talk much. All he does is walk around and grunt. The teachers try to promote him to speak and say what he is thinking but all he does is grunt. What can you learn about to better understand how to reach this boy?

Personal and Professional Literacy Resources

- Pressley, M. (2006). *Reading Instruction that Works: The Case for Balanced Teaching.* New York: Guilford Press. This book focuses on current research and practice in classrooms that emphasize balanced literacy approaches. The chapters focus on key aspects of *No Child Left Behind* and *Reading First Initiatives.* What I have found useful about this resource is the wealth of research-based literacy recommendations that all teachers can follow in order to improve their instruction and enhance student learning and motivation.

- Garmston, R. (2005). *The Presenter's Fieldbook.* Norwood, MA: Christopher-Gordon Publishers. Teachers who want to learn how to develop more effective presentation skills will find this fieldbook valuable in many ways. The chapters are logically organized around strategies to deliver effective presentations. Those who plan professional development opportunities will find the format of this book practical.

- Painter, K. (2006). *Living and Teaching the Writing Workshop.* Portsmouth, NH: Heinemann. I have always used writing or journaling as an effective method to gain more knowledge about my own insights related to literacy instruction. This book is one of my favorite resources because it guides the reader through the writing process and offers practical recommendations on how to reflect more deeply on instruction using writing as a tool. In addition, the second part of this book is devoted to helping teachers integrate the writing process in their own classrooms.

Goal #6: Collegiality

Teacher Fosters Positive Collaboration with School and Community

> *"Strange as our situation here upon earth. Each of us comes for a short visit, not knowing why, yet sometimes seeming to divine a purpose. From the standpoint of daily life, however, there is one thing we do know: that man is here for the sake of other men."*
>
> —Albert Einstein

Journaling Thoughts on Collegiality

Why do you want to make a commitment to the learning behavior of collegiality? Why will achieving this goal have an influence on instruction?

Thoughts for Group Discussion:

Self-Reflection: Making a Commitment

Goal Rationale:

Based on standards by literacy organizations, it is an expectation that teachers work collegially with adults about the well-being of students and are willing to work together with other professionals to improve the learning environment in the school and community.

According to *Webster's* dictionary, collegiality was defined as the cooperative relationship of others. To be collegial means power of authority vested equally or a mark of camaraderie with others. To acquire the literacy goal of collegiality really requires the ability to be humble in all situations and to embrace a modest spirit. Working with others is all situations can be difficult. I have noticed that as a teacher and professor, for some it just seems to come naturally for some people. This might be a distinguishing attribute of their personal gifts and talents. For others, the disposition of collegiality and the ability to foster positive collaboration needs cultivation.

When I think about my positive and negative experiences when working with others, I recall the positive ones were experiences where my thoughts and ideas were valued. I enjoy working with peers who value my opinion. I think students are the same way. They want to know if their teacher values their opinion and the work they do. This is just human nature.

When I think about how we learn skills to develop collegiality, I think about the early experiences I had as a child when we used to play in the sand box in our back yard. Because we were the only large family in the neighborhood with four kids in our family, all the other children would come to our house and play in our sandbox. I learned to not throw sand. In real life when working with others, I have learned to apply this lesson by not throwing negative attitudes to other group members but instead to foster relationships built on trust. If I threw sand at my friends, they would cry and leave.

There have been moments when I have worked in groups when I felt like crying and leaving because someone was being so cruel. I recall being in a collaborative group where I was the leader and a senior member of the group, put me down in front of others. Not only did this make me feel bad, but it caused others to question their confidence in me.

What does it mean that we are here for the sake of other men? What does collegiality mean to you? How do you feel when working with others that have the same goal? How do you feel when working with others that might have a different agenda than your own? When I was researching the dispositions related to reading and writing, there was a lot of emphasis placed on getting along with others, working with peers, collaborating, and maintaining positive relationships. Teacher dispositions on working with others from teacher and literacy associations read as follows:

- The teacher candidate meets or exceeds evaluation of professional competencies in personal qualities and relationships with others

- The teacher works with colleagues to observe, and provide feedback on each other's practice
- The teacher fosters relationships with school colleagues, parents, and agencies in the larger community to support students learning and well-being

I wanted the title of this chapter to express the value of literacy teachers' ability to have positive collaborative relationships. I struggled to find a word that was all encompassing and one that communicated the common goal of showing genuine respect for others. Words such as camaraderie, collaboration, relationships, teamwork, and cooperation did not emphasize the importance of this disposition. Following is a summary of how theory and practice support the literacy goal of collegiality.

It was not until a very important peer told me a story about "school culture" that I started to think differently about what it actually means to foster positive collaboration. He had me think about family in relationship with school culture and to paraphrase influenced me to think differently about how [The school is our family and how we work with them represents our ability to be collegial.]. In my mind, I thought, "The school is my family and each member of the family is equally important and should be respected in the same manner." The metaphor of school and family and the word collegiality stuck with me for a long time. No one had ever really talked about collegiality with me before, so the professor's insight shaped the way I think about collaboration and positive peer relationships.

Since collegiality is difficult to measure, the research available focuses more on beliefs and attitudes of literacy teachers related to school culture, peer collaborations, and parental relationships. In the opening quote by Albert Einstein, literacy teachers can realize "that man is here for the sake of other men." One question derived from this quote can be, "what kinds of contributions can teachers from their literacy experiences make that will benefit other literacy teachers?"

Recently I was reading *Chronicle of Higher Education* and I noticed an advertisement for a book that looked particularly interesting. The book that caught my attention was *Into the Classroom: Developing the Scholarship of Teaching and Learning* by Hatch (2006). I was unfamiliar with the author but I was very familiar with The Carnegie Foundation for the Advancement of Teaching, the association supporting the book. As I read the book, I read about the contributions of four teachers and I began to think differently about what it means to foster positive collaborations. Boerst, Cone, Moore, and Wolk are teachers who take a different approach to building collegiality. The author describes their actions as ones that go beyond the learning of their students.

Collectively these four teachers have 55 years of teaching experience. In addition, they are well respected in their school community. Their impact on others is shaped by their humble disposition that power, authority, and control does not influence change, but the ability to use one's experiences to shape ideas for different audiences. They also seek personal and public inquiries on how to improve teaching. Through interactions with colleagues, they share experiences to enlighten others practice, as well as their own. Some of these interactions include:

- Analyzing instructional videos to deal with issues or problems in the classroom
- Started Teacher Research Groups as a way of continuing conversations about practice
- Working with public officials to create new policies
- Identify influential researchers to gain knowledge and inspire writing
- Communicate ideas in national venues to inform a wider audience of colleagues
- Engage in reflective examination of their own practice and document so others can learn
- Network with teachers in other schools to gain new perspectives
- Lend books and resources that other teachers might not encounter
- Informal sharing of lessons and ideas in hallways and faculty discussions

One prominent school educator, Gertrude Williams, who is a retired principal and teacher of 49 years in the Baltimore public schools, fostered positive collaborations. Gertrude Williams achieved the literacy goal of collegiality by valuing collaboration and conversing about meaningful school issues with the *entire* school community. Robinson documents Williams's strategies for building positive collaborations in her book, *Education as My Agenda: Gertrude Williams, Race, and the Baltimore Public Schools* published in 2005 by Palgrave Macmillian.

In this biography, the author describes one of Williams' hallmarks as the ability to cultivate an intricate web with students, staff, students' families, the school's immediate neighbors, and friends of the school from far and wide (p. 99). Some of the ways she built collaborations with parents that I thought were valuable and ones that can be modeled by all teachers are:

- Speaking with parents during all hours of the day
- Supporting teacher-parent school events such as potluck suppers, talent shows, and fix-up day
- Recruited parents to be part of the school staff to strengthen the tie between school and community
- Reinforced parent-staff-community partnerships by inviting and being invited to local day care centers
- Encouraged talented parents to pursue degrees in education
- Started the Fund for Educational Excellence to raise money for school initiatives

As documented by Robinson, Gertrude Williams not only valued positive collaborations with everyone but she made it her mantra, which is most likely a factor in her success with student achievement. Williams acknowledges in a closing comment that education is everyone's business.

> I didn't become an educator for wealth or glamour. The rewards of taking education as my agenda have come from helping children develop into competent and capable citizens....I run into parents who tell me what their child is doing, and they'll say, "And it all started at Barclay." Of course, it didn't *all* start there. But I'm proud that we did our part. (Robinson, 2005, 210)

Table 6.1   Negative Factors that Decrease Collegiality Checklist

_____	1. Lack of knowledge about group goals or topics being discussed.
_____	2. Respect for group members due to seniority beliefs.
_____	3. A disrespect for cultural barriers that decrease ability to function harmoniously.
_____	4. Being requested to participate when you do not want to.
_____	5. Feelings of isolation within school community.
_____	6. Rumors about people who you do not trust.
_____	7. Closeness of school community and a lack of inclusion with new faculty.
_____	8. Factors related to personal issues such as religious beliefs.
_____	9. Conflict with pedagogical beliefs.
_____	10. Overwhelming amount of expectations and workload with minimal support.
_____	11. Other Factors

Review the list and reflect on the negative factors you have checked. Do you notice any trends with your responses? Are their other factors that need to be considered?

_____

_____

_____

_____

_____

_____

Observation from a Window into Literacy Lives

Working with others is an important part of one's ability to be successful in any situation. One of my biggest concerns is with those in leadership roles who might take advantage of others to manipulate how others feel about a group member. I recall an experience that happened to me when I had been having many negative encounters with a particular group member and leader. On one occasion, I realized that she was reporting to higher authority false information about me. I really did not know how to handle this. I respected my peers but I did not understand why this person did not come to me first to discuss the concerns. A meeting was requested to discuss our differences. Because I wanted our meeting to be communicated accurately to the school leader, I decided to invite a secretary to take notes during the meeting. I was waiting for the meeting to begin and decided to get something to drink. When I returned the individual I was to meet with was in my room waiting for me. The secretary I had invited never showed up so I continued the meeting. After the meeting, I ran into the secretary and she apologized for not being at the meeting but she was told she was not needed by the person I was meeting with. I did not understand why someone would send someone away that I invited to the meeting and not tell me about it. This situation was very concerning to me and I just could not believe this happened. When I reflect on this situation, I try to think about actions I could have done differently. I also think about how important it is to be collegial no matter what. I realized that I did do the right things later. I tried to resolve the issue with the person. I tried to protect myself by asking someone else to attend the meeting.

Self-questioning to Achieve Goal

Self-questioning to Achieve Goal

What challenges do you experience that keeps you from being collegial?

How Colleagues Overcome Challenges:

Having the disposition of collegiality can be achieved with a positive attitude about collaboration, not just with peers you enjoy working with, but with all your colleagues and with the larger school community. How would you evaluate your level of collegiality? What is getting in the way of your ability to foster positive collaborations?

What statements on the *Teacher Recognizes Collegiality as Essential Checklist* did you find difficult to answer? What actions related to developing positive collaborations have room for growth? How do others in your school environment feel about collegiality? How do members of your school community demonstrate that they value positive collaborations? Reflecting on some of your beliefs will help you identify factors that might be keeping you from experiencing collegiality in your school and with colleagues, parents, and the school community. When I reflect on my beliefs, I realize several things:

- Collegiality is something I value
- I need to consider others' perspectives when making critical decisions
- Parents should be equally respected and valued
- Communicating concerns early in a difficult situation is important
- Trust your instincts and invite others to be present if you do not feel comfortable
- Parents deserve to be treated in a positive manner regardless of matters that we disagree on
- Document your concerns
- When you feel you have tried everything, do not blame yourself
- Consider that the environment you are in is not a healthy one and work on finding an alternative solution

Colleagues are not just those people to whom you are very close. Colleagues are everyone within the school-family environment. Depending on your teaching situation, there might be barriers that are unique to you. By keeping in mind some of the main ideas that contribute to achieving the literacy goal of collegiality, will you focus on formulating an effective and attainable plan. Let us review the following tenets:

- Collegiality is a belief that power of authority is vested equally
- Collegiality is a mark of camaraderie or friendship with others
- Collegiality really requires the ability to be humble in all situations
- Collegiality is embraced with a modest spirit

A Sense of Acceptance

When power is established by roles or titles, members of collaborative groups might feel inferior. Control related to decision making can paralyze problem solving, idea generating, or critical thinking. Participation from all group members becomes minimal if voices are not valued.

The ability to be collegial in collaborative groups is characterized by a sense of community. Community can be established when groups are formed. Codes of conduct can be discussed so members know how to act or react. Change in attitude when in a collaborative situation that is not healthy can get you closer to a more collegial relationship. Think about what it is that you can change right now that will improve rapport with your colleagues. Ask yourself some questions, How well do I listen to others' point of view? What is making me feel inferior? Am I making others feel like they have no authority? Sometimes students also face this same sense of inferiority when working with others. To learn more about how students feel about working with others, administer the Collaborative Group Inventory in Table 6.2.

Table 6.2   Collaborative Group Inventory

1. What are the attitudes of the group members?

2. What strengths can you bring to help your group achieve their goal?

3. What issues do you foresee that might keep your group from working together?

4. What are positive actions you can take to be collegial in your school or group?

5. Do you believe your colleagues consider you collegial? If so, how? If not, why not?

No Time for Sharing or Collaborating

Time is always an issue for teachers. Using time wisely during group discussions can help you be more effective as a group. Keeping on task and topic helps monitor time. People who tend to get off track need strategies to help them self-monitor their participation in relationship to group goals.

There are several strategies that groups can use to utilize time wisely.

- Provide all members with a questionnaire about what do they want to gain from the group
- Prepare a mission statement or set of values for the group
- Determine meeting locations in advance so as to minimize confusion and email correspondence
- Discuss procedures for off task conversations, such as writing down the stories or ideas in a book to be read at the end of the group meeting
- Start and end on time with pre-planned goals
- Use traveling notebooks (Allington & Cunningham, 2006). Traveling notebooks can be used to share knowledge from teacher-to-teacher prior to collaborations, in order to identify major points of discussion in advance.
- Invite everyone to end with positive statements or future goals for the next meeting

Dealing with Incompatible Personalities Effectively

Occasionally one member of the group is a person with whom you simply do not get along. Sometimes this is due to factors outside of your control. For example, group members who do not value collegiality or use title as a power tool. On other occasions, the group leader may lack the knowledge or skills to be an effective leader.

Learning more about yourself is a way to overcome situations in which you are forced to deal with personalities that clash with your own. Personalities that are not compatible can be a major factor of group success. Learning style assessments that you can administer yourself will help you understand more about your own personality or learning styles. A free on-line resource that you can take to identify multiple intelligence styles is www.mitest.com. This assessment is quick and easy to use. After answering a series of questions, the computer can evaluate your multiple intelligence. Another assessment that I recommend for teachers and students is *Learning Styles Inventory* (Renzulli, Rizza, & Smith, 2002). This assessment evaluates abilities, interests, and styles in the act of learning.

In this section, you have been introduced to new strategies and ideas on how to achieve the goal of collegiality. You have been asked to think differently about what collaboration means to you. Take a few minutes to formulate a plan on how you can achieve the goal of fostering positive collaborations in your literacy-teaching situation.

 Challenges I face that influence my ability to be collegial are:

_____

_____

_____

_____

_____

_____

_____

_____

_____

_____

_____

_____

Positive solutions I can take to be collegial in my community are:

_____

_____

_____

_____

_____

_____

_____

_____

_____

_____

_____

_____

Self-evaluation of Progress

Self-evaluation of Progress

Have you achieved your goal? If not, what positive action can you take to achieve the goal?

New Ideas:

This chapter focuses on helping you come closer to achieving the literacy goal of collegiality, as teachers fostering peer collaboration in schools, with parents and colleagues and with the larger school community is important. With that in mind, the three goals of this chapter that helped you realize achieving the literacy goal of collegiality were:

- Understand your strengths and areas for improvement when working with others
- Learn about factors that weaken collegiality in school environments

- Reflect on your actions when working with others
- Identify behaviors that negatively impact your ability to be collegial with others
- Learn effective strategies to foster positive collaboration

Teachers are faced with many challenges for the sake of the common good of helping children be successful. Beliefs, attitudes, perceptions, and even personal characteristics play a role in how well the goal of collegiality can be achieved. In the words of Palmer, we can learn that a civic model of building positive relationships is not only civil but merits a deeper integration into the culture of schools and within the hearts of teachers. Palmer brings to light the value of collegiality by stating:

> The community envisioned by the civic model is one of public mutuality rather than personal vulnerability…learn to share a common territory and common resources, to resolve mutual conflicts and mutual problems. In civic community, we may not learn what is on each others' hearts, but we learn that if we do not hang together, we will hang separately. (Palmer, 1998, p. 92)

What can you learn about yourself when reflecting on this quote by Palmer? What can you learn about the literacy goal of collegiality? What has helped you develop a renewed motivation to seek collegial relationships in your school community? What can you make as higher goals as a literacy teacher that will also benefit students?

When I reflect on the Palmer quote above, I think about what it means to be a civic community. Sometimes, I think we forget that it is very important to be civil to others. We have to remember to respect their opinion and their unique differences. I realize this is not easy to do with all people, but if I make an effort to do so, I will feel better. I also feel more confident about how I act in public. My greatest fear is working with a group of people who do not value my opinions or my level of expertise. Parker reminds me to work on strategies to effectively resolve conflicts. One suggestion a former principal recommended to me prior to a difficult meeting was to settle the disagreement by having a win-win situation for both parties. My principal reminded me that we have our school standards and our personal standards, but the parent also has their standards, as well as needs and you need to consider both sides, not just your own.

My personal goal that will allow me to be develop collegial behaviors is:

_____

_____

_____

_____

_____

_____

_____

_____

_____

_____

_____

_____

_____

_____

_____

The reason this goal is important to me is:

_____

_____

_____

_____

_____

_____

_____

_____

_____

_____

_____

_____

_____

_____

Wonderful, you are getting closer to appreciating what it means to be collegial. Use the following checklist to help you evaluate your goal.

Self-monitoring Checklist

Self-monitoring Statement	Behaviors you Display	Behavioral Changes to Consider
How do you demonstrate your positive collaborative relationships?		
What effective strategies do you use to improve on collegiality in your school situation?		
What behaviors do you possess that weaken your ability to be collegial?		
Recall a time when you felt you were not working well with others and you did not like certain decisions that were being made. What did you do?		
If you are upset with a colleague, how would you react?		

Teaching Ideas for the Literacy Classroom

My Thoughts on Teaching Enthusiasm

Now you want to help your students be more enthusiastic about reading and writing. What can you do to help them achieve this goal?

How will you invite students to set individual goals to achieve Enthusiasm in Reading and Writing:

To achieve the goal of collegiality by fostering positive collaborations with others, implement some of the following strategies. In addition, encourage students to follow some of the same practices when working in collaborative groups.

Collegiality Guidelines

Establish collaboration goals with the group prior to working together on an important project. For example, your guidelines may include the following

- Speak privately with peers who you feel clash with your own personality and establish personal collegial goals on how to work peacefully together
- Express concerns immediately to reduce miscommunication or false perceptions
- Be observant when working with others and pay attention to behaviors that signal concerns
- When difficult situations arise, avoid taking negative stances but present positive alternatives to achieving group goals
- Do not be afraid to speak what is on your mind
- Exhibit behaviors that demonstrate they value and appreciate everyone in the group
- Avoid talking negatively about collegial relationships with others in public or in private encounters

Mighty Mission Statements

Mission statements are a great way to establish literacy goals of the committee. I recommend they be established during the first meeting. I have used mission statements at the beginning of the school year with my students. A Sample mission statement follows. More mission statements that teachers can use in the classroom or with groups can be found in *Collaborative Literacy* by Israel, Sisk, and Block (2005).

Mission Statement

The mission of the group is to establish literacy goals for the forthcoming year based on high academic standards that meet the needs of all students in the school community as well as promote a values-based learning model that incorporates character traits with strong literacy goals.

The goal of this chapter was to get you to think differently about what it means to foster positive collaborations with others and the reason for doing so. You are on your way to achieving the goal of collegiality. Teachers need to be able to trust one another enough to share ideas and their struggles, too. In order to seek support and help from their colleagues, teachers need to nurture collegial relationships. It is equally important for the leaders within the school community to also expect teachers to be collegial and model this behavior as well. Learning about ourselves and our relationship habits is very important as I have tried to point out.

Teachers Thinking Deeply

Following is a list of questions and professional development resources that are recommended to teachers who want to reflect deeply on their instructional practices in reading and writing.

Discussion Questions to Maintain and Extend Goal

1. Discuss situations that were positive and negative experiences about collegial relationships and develop strategies on how to deal more effectively with others.

2. What areas such as leadership, teacher research, or collaboration within schools and classrooms can you learn more about to understand what research says about building collegiality?

3. What issues do you face in your school community that influence your relationship with others?

4. What issues do you face with your students that keep them from developing positive collaborative relationships? What are some positive solutions that you can take to positively address some of these issues?

Real-life Scenario

You were hired to teach a specific grade. Once you started your teaching assignment, you became aware that you are now the literacy coordinator of your school. When you signed your contract, you were unaware of this position. You are now expected to be the leader and manage an entire group of older teachers you are working with. This is your first year as the teacher and you do not know what you are doing. You have many problems but the one that bothers you the most is when a colleague shows you disrespect during a meeting and humiliates you. How do you react to this issue?

Personal and Professional Literacy Resources

Following is a list of books that I recommend to teachers who want to reflect deeply on their ability to be collegial. These resources focus on developing a variety of collaborative group strategies, as well as offer assistance with additional self-help strategies.

- Seabrook, J. (2004). *Fury Logic: A Guide to Life's Little Challenges.* Hong Kong: Seabrook Publishing, Ltd. This little book can be used to start group meetings and reinforce the behaviors that are defined by the literacy goal of collegiality in an inspirational and humorous manner.

- Tutu, D. M. (1997). *No Future Without Forgiveness.* New York: Doubleday. Unfortunately, not all relationships are collegial. This book focuses on the idea of forgiveness. This book is important to me because I have learned that we need to forgive those who have offended us and this book illustrates that point very well. This book can also be used as a read aloud in the classroom to encourage students to develop collegial relationships that will last them a lifetime.

- Robinson, J. (2005). *Education as my Agenda: Gertrude Williams, Race and the Baltimore Public Schools.* New York: Palgrave MacMillan. This book is for those who work with others on a daily basis and how to develop the literacy goal of collegiality by thinking differently about the influence of culture and community in building collegial relationships.

- Edwards, J. A., & Hamilton, E. W. (2003). *Simeon's Gift*. New York: Harper Collins Publishers. This is a lovely picture book that talks about discovering the challenges of life and how to overcome them by building bridges with others. Use this book as a motivational tool to help you reflect more deeply on what collegiality means in your life or as a read-aloud with students to foster the development of collegiality in the classroom.

Closing Reflections

Enriching the Future of Teaching and Literacy Learning

"Let him who knows which seeds will grow, speak then to me."

—Shakespeare

Congratulations, you have successfully reflected on six literacy goals that are within the core of the heart of exemplary literacy teachers. An analogy that you can think about related Shakespeare's quote and discovering which seeds will grow as you begin transforming your teaching heart is similar to those of a farmer who plants seeds and watches them grow to see which one will grow fastest, tallest, and strongest. The actions a farmer takes to help make sure all his plants grow are in direct relationship with the nature of crops he wants to harvest. If the farmer waters his crops, he will have a fruitful harvest. The heart of the teacher is at the core of what makes an exemplary teacher. One of my favorite conversations is from a very famous book called *Alice in Wonderland* by Carroll, which summarizes the challenges that lie ahead for those who seek something new.

"Would you tell me please, which way I ought to go?

"That depends on where you want to get to," said the cat.

"I don't much care where-" said Alice.

"Then it doesn't matter which way you go," said the cat.

"-so long as I get somewhere," said Alice.

"Oh, you're sure to do that," said the cat, "If you only keep walking."

—Lewis Carroll, Alice in Wonderland

Seeking a new way of behaving brings new levels of challenges and professionalism that depends on different factors, which may lead to different directions. The directions that you take could be influenced by different factors, such as personal beliefs, internal or external controls, or political agendas. The purpose of this chapter is to help you take actions that you have decided to change regarding your personal inner teaching emotions at the heart of teaching in order to achieve exemplary literacy instruction. In this chapter, you will learn how literacy goals can be applied into everyday classroom issues and instruction. The focus of this book has raised awareness about your dispositions related to literacy instruction. Through the stories, self-reflection, and discussions you have learned to:

- *Enrich Personal and Professional Life*
- *Reflect on Effective Literacy Instruction*
- *Organize Classroom Instruction Around Literacy Goals*

Inspirational Professionals Who Help Me Discover My Purpose in Life

Jewel, which is a pseudonym, was in graduate school to obtain a certification in elementary teaching. I noticed something about Jewel on the first day of class, when I met her. Jewel arrived early and sat up front. The co-professor and I were busy getting the classroom ready and noticed that she had arrived. After welcoming her to our class, she wanted to know what kinds of books second grade students liked best. During class she was not shy about participating, but did so without seeming too arrogant about her level of knowledge.

When we did group activities she was usually selected as the spokesperson and it was obvious her peers respected her. During class one day, membership information to belong to the International Reading Association was distributed. Jewel brought in her check and membership application the next class period and was the only student to do so. She continued to contact me after the semester ended for information about teaching phonics or research related to reading instruction. Jewel's level of professionalism exceeded all graduate students that semester and every semester since she was in my class. This was evident in her need to seek knowledge about topics of interest, her ability to work with others in a collaborative environment, her willingness to participate in literacy associations, her interest in seeking answers or direction on literacy instruction in and out of class, and her ability to do so without arrogance or false pride.

According to Block and Mangieri (2003), an exemplary literacy teacher is "an individual who provided instruction in reading and writing in an outstanding manner" (p. 1). Jewel's inner professional qualities eventually allowed her to become an outstanding second grade teacher. Moreover, the children in the under-resourced class in which she taught, thought she did so with a special love and compassion.

Many practicing teachers exhibit the same level of professionalism as Jewel and are driven to becoming outstanding literacy teachers. Pressley and his research team (2006), when investigating effective whole school environments, found that the very best teachers never believed they had reached their goal and were always in pursuit of it.

By reflecting on practice, documenting and telling stories about effective instruction, teachers learn to participate in a richer dialogue that influences personal and professional growth. I have always learned from asking questions about teaching decision making when it comes to understanding how the very best teachers of literacy construct their inner craft of teaching.

You might think that this book is about teaching from the heart rather than the mind. To me it is about teaching with the mind, heart, and soul. Each of the six literacy goals are highlighted with stories that have changed my way of feeling and thinking. Some of the stories about teaching are perhaps embarrassing, while others are humorous and heartfelt. All of the stories have shaped who I am as a teacher. It is your teaching story that you carry in your heart that will also shape you as a teacher and guide you to achieve the literacy goals of exemplary teachers.

In this book, you have focused on beliefs and attitudes of effective teachers who are enthusiastic about reading and writing and demonstrate this pure love with their students, regardless of their content area. Through reflection and self-assessment, you have learned how reading and writing become the links to aid the teacher in meeting each unique student's desire for learning based on the personal interests of the student and their individual styles of learning. You have discovered more about what it is that you love about reading and writing. You have also documented strategies that you can take to the classroom that can help you be more enthusiastic about your love of reading and writing.

When I reflect on how difficult it was for me to write this book and how many times I struggled to communicate my message, I think about the many students who also struggle in school. It was not easy for me to synthesize my years of experiences, my knowledge, and my philosophy in a way that is easy to understand. I live my teaching life. I have tried to invite you to experience that life but you can never fully experience what I have because we are on different teaching journeys.

When I think about some of the decisions I have made regarding how students receive information about assignments or projects that are due in the classroom. One of the things I have learned over the years is that the way teachers communicate information and the manner in which students receive information about what they are to learn has a significant impact on how receptive they are about doing work. Getting students to be motivated about doing work is a high priority for me. When making decisions about what types of assignments I need to give to my students, I have to consider the overall learning outcome that I want to achieve. Thinking in this manner also forces me to think about how I am going to present the material, assignment, or the expectation to my students. How will I assess it and why? How will I work with my peers to achieve my goal. The goals in this book are goals that I truly believe will help you be the very best literacy teacher you can be. Are there other dispositions that you can possess to make you an exemplary teacher. I am sure there are and I invite the readers of this book to find them and write about them so others can benefit from them.

One recommendation I want to make before we end our dispositions journey together is to make sure you are passionate about what you are doing and want to do. I have never been successful or very enthusiastic about teaching from curriculum that is not my own. In order for me to be enthusiastic in front of the students about the assignments, I need to make them my own and construct them in a way that fits the needs of my students. This has been the most important lesson I have learned while writing this book. When I stumbled for words, I looked in other books for ideas on how I could improve my writing. When I struggled with organization, I kept revising until my reviewers felt the book was well organized and easy to read. When I struggle with teaching, I try to look for ways to improve my practice. I am passionate about being a better teacher, and a better writer, and a better person. Make teaching your own and do it with passion.

Establishing New Goals for the Future

Now that you have achieved your goals, what goals can you set for future personal growth?

My New Ideas:

References

Allen, J. (2006). *Becoming a literacy leader: Supporting learning and change.* Portland, ME: Stenhouse Publishers.

Allington, R. L. & Cunningham, P. M. (2007). *Schools that work: Where all children read and write.* New York: Allyn and Bacon.

Allington, R. L. & McGill-Franzen, A. (2004). Looking Back, Looking Forward: A Conversation About Teaching Reading in the 21st Century. In Ruddell, R. B., & Unrau, N. J. (2004). *Theoretical models and processes of reading.* (5th ed.). Newark, DE: International Reading Association, pp. 5–32.

Baker, L. (2005). Developmental differences in metacognition: Implications for metacognitively oriented reading instruction. In Israel, S. E., Block, C. C., Bauserman, K., & Kinnucan-Welsch, K. (2005). *Metacognition in literacy learning: Theory, assessment, instruction, and professional development.* Maywah, NJ: Erlbaum, pp. 61–79.

Bain, K. (2004). *What the best college teachers do.* Cambridge, MA: Harvard University Press.

Baum, F. L. (1993). *The wizard of Oz.* Ware: Hertfordshire: Wordsworth Editions Ltd.

Block, C. C., & Israel, S. E. (in press). *Quotes to inspire great reading teachers: A reflective tool to aid you in advancing student's literacy.* San Francisco, CA: Corwin Press.

Block, C. C., & Israel, S. E. (2005). *Reading first and beyond: A guidebook for teachers and literacy coaches.* San Francisco, CA: Corwin Press.

Block, C. C., Israel, S. E. (2006). *Quotes to inspire great reading teachers: A reflective tool for advancing students' literacy.* Thousand Oaks, CA: Corwin Press.

Block, C. C., & Mangieri, J. N. (2003). *Exemplary literacy teachers: Promoting success for all children in grades K–5.* New York: Guilford Press.

Block, C. C., Oakar, M.m & Hurt, N. (2002). The expertise of literacy teachers: A continuum from preschool to Grade 5. *Reading Research Quarterly, 37,* 2, 178–206.

Carroll, L. (1993). *Alice in Wonderland.* Ware: Hertfordshire: Wordsworth Editions Limited.

Cochran-Smith, M., & Zeichner, K. (2005). *Studying teacher education: The report of the AERA Panel on Research and Teacher Education.* Mahwah, NJ: Erlbaum.

Demi. (2001). *Gandhi.* New York: Margaret K. McElderry Books.

Dewey, J. (1902, 1915, 2001). *The school and society and the child and the curriculum.* New York, Mineola: Dover Publications. (Original publication in 1902 & Revised in 1915 by University of Chicago Press, Chicago, IL)

Drew, T. & Tande, K. (Retrieved 2006). *NCATE dispositions standards implementation survey.* Washington, DC: NCATE, http://www.hpcnet.org/peru/schoolprofessionalstudies/ncate

Drucker, M. J. (2003). What reading teachers should know about ESL learners. *The Reading Teacher, 57, (1),* 22–29.

Edmunds, K. M., & Bauserman, K. L. (2006). What teachers can learn about reading motivation through conversations with children. *The Reading Teacher, 59, 414–424.*

Fitzgerald, J. (2000) How will bilingual/ESL programs in literacy change in the next millennium. *Reading Research Quarterly,* 35, 520.

Foster, K. K. (2004). Warming up to learn: Using introductory questions to activate critical thinking. *Thinking Classroom, 5 (4), 38–43.*

Flavell, J. (1979). Metacognition and cognitive monitoring: A new era of cognitive developmental inquiry. *American Psychologist,* 34 (10), 906–911.

Garcia, G. E. (2000) How will bilingual/ESL programs in literacy change in the next millennium. *Reading Research Quarterly,* 35, 521.

Great Professional Development Quotes. http//www.teachermentors.com. Retrieved on June 29, 2006 Best Practices Resources: Great Professional Development Quotes.

Harris, T. L., & Hodges, R. E. (1995). *The Literacy Dictionary: The vocabulary of reading and writing.* Newark, DE: International Reading Association.

Hatch, T. (2006). *Into the classroom: Developing the scholarship of teaching and learning.* San Francisco, CA: Jossey-Bass.

Heart Quotes. www.heartquotes.net/Wisdom.html. Retreived on June 29, 2006.

INTASC Principles (Interstate New Teachers Assessment and Support Consortium).

Israel, S. E. (2004). Personal Communication dated July, 24, 2004. Fishers, Indiana.

Israel, S. E., Bauserman, K. L., & Block, C. C. (2005). Metacognitive Assessment Strategies. *Thinking Classroom,* 6 (2), 21–28.

Israel, S. E., Block, C. C., Bauserman, K., & Kinnucan-Welsch, K. (2005). *Metacognition in literacy learning: Theory, assessment, instruction, and professional development.* Mahwah, NJ: Erlbaum.

Israel, S. E. & Monaghan, J. E. (2007). *Early Reading Pioneers.* Newark, NJ: International Reading Association.

Israel, S. E., Sisk, D., & Block, C. C. (2006). *Collaborative Literacy: Engaging Strategies for All students.* San Francisco, CA: Corwin Press.

Jaménez, R. T. & Barrera, R. (2000). How will bilingual/ESL programs in literacy change in the next millennium. *Reading Research Quarterly,* 35, 522–523.

Jaménez, R. T., Smith, P. H., & Martinex-León, N. (2003). Freedom and form: The language and literacy practices to two Mexican schools. *Reading Research Quarterly, 38,* 488–508.

Jones, D. (200?). *Celebrate what's right about the world.* Windsor, CA: Dewitt Jones Productions.

LeadershipNow.com.   http://www.leadershipnow.com/leadersshipquotes.html Retreived on June 29, 2006.

Leslie, L., & Caldwell, J. (2006) *Qualitative Reading Inventory-4.* New York: Allyn & Bacon.

Mahiri, J. (2000). What will be the social implications and interactions of schooling in the next millennium? *Reading Research Quarterly,* 35, 422–423.

Mish, FEditor in Chief (Do I list all the names? (2004). Merriam-Webster's Collegiate Dictionary, 11th ed. Springfield, MA: Merriam-Webster, Incorporated.

Muth, J. (2002). *The Three Questions.* New York: Scholastic.

National Council for Accreditation of Teacher Education. (2002, Revised 2006). *Professional Standards for the Accreditation of Schools, Colleges, and Departments of Education.* Washington, DC: NCATE.

National Institute of Child Health and Human Development. (2000). *Report of the National Reading Panel: Teaching Children to Read: Report of the Subgroups* (00-4754). Washington, DC: U.S. Government Printing Office.

Neuman, S. B. & Celano, D. (2006). The knowledge gap: Implications of leveling the playing field for low-income and middle-income children. *Reading Research Quarterly, 41, 176–201.*

Palmer, P. (2004). *A hidden wholeness.* San Francisco, CA: Jossey-Bass.

Paris, S. G., & Stahl, S. (2005). *Children's reading comprehension and assessment.* Mahwah, NJ: Lawrence Erlbaum Associates.

Palmer, P. (1998). *The Courage to Teach: Exploring the inner landscape of a teacher's life.* San Francisco, CA: Jossey-Bass, pp. 163–183.

Polacco, P. (1998). *Thank you, Mr. Falker.* New York: Philomel Books.

Pressley, M. (2006, April 29). *What the future of reading research could be.* Paper presented at the International Reading Association's Reading Research Conference 2006, Chicago, Illinois.

Pressley, M., Dolezal, S. E., Raphael, L. M., Mohan, L., Roehrig, A. D., & Bogner, K. (2003). *Motivating primary-grade students.* New York: Guilford Press.

Powell-Brown, A. (2004). Can you be a teacher of literacy if you don't love to read? *Journal of Adolescent and Adult Literacy, 47,* 284–288.

Professional Standards and Ethics Committee of the International Reading Association (Revised 2003). *Standards for reading professionals: A reference for the preparation of educators in the united states.* Newark, DE: International Reading Association.

Purcell-Gates, V. (2000). What will be the social implications and interactions of schooling in the next millennium? *Reading Research Quarterly, 35,* 421–422.

Reynolds, P. H. (2004). *Ish.* New York: Candlewick Press.

Renzulli, J. S., Rizza, M. G., & Smith, L. H. (2002). *Learning styles inventory: A measure of student preferences for instructional techniques. Version III.* Mansfield Center, CT: Creative Learning Press, Inc.

Rogers, T. (2000). What will be the social implications and interactions of schooling in the next millennium? *Reading Research Quarterly, 35,* 420.

Robinson, J. (2005). *Education as My Agenda: Gertrude Williams, Race, and the Baltimore Public Schools.* New York: Palgrave Macmillian.

Ruddell, R. B., & Unrau, N. J. (2004). *Theoretical models and processes of reading,* 5th ed. Newark, DE: International Reading Association.

Saint-Exupéry, A. (1971). *The Little Prince.* New York: A Harvest/ HBJBook.

Sanacore, J. (2004). Genuine caring and literacy learning for African American children. *The Reading Teacher, 57,* 744–753.

Shaw, M. D. (2003). *Ten amazing people: And how they changed the world.* Woodstock, VT: Skylight Paths Publishing.

Schunk, D. H. (2000). Learning theories: An educational perspective.Upper Saddle River, NJ: Prentice-Hall, Inc.

Standards for Reading Professionals. (Revised 2003). *A reference for the preparation of educators in the United States.* Newark, DE: International Reading Association.

Strommen, L. T. & Mates, B.F. (2004). Learning to love reading: Interviews with older children and teens. *Journal of Adolescent and Adult Literacy,* 48, 188–200.

Svoboda, M. (2000). *Abundant treasures: Meditations on the many gifts of the spirit.* Mystic, CT: Twenty-Third Publications.

Sweet, A. P. & Snow, C. E. (2003). *Rethinking reading comprehension.* New York: Guilford Press.

Think Exist. http://en.thinkexist.com/quotations. Retrieved on June 23, 2006.

Weiner, H. & Cohen, A. R. (2003). *Dispositions in Teacher Education Programs: An Opportunity for Reform.* Paper presented at the Second Annual National Conference on Teaching Dispositions. November 19 at Eastern Kentucky University, Richmond Kentucky.

Index

About the Author

Susan E. Israel, PhD is a Literacy Consultant for Burkhart Network, LLC in Indianapolis, Indiana. Dr. Israel conducts research in preschool literacy, organizes and manages projects, creates new materials, collaborates with colleagues from universities, and guides literacy production. Previously, she taught in the Alliance for Catholic Education at the University of Notre Dame. In addition, she was the 2005 Panhellenic Outstanding Professor of the Year at the University of Dayton.

Other Books for Teachers by This Author

Early Reading First and Beyond (2008)

Handbook of Research on Reading Comprehension (2008)

Metacognitive Assessment Tools (2007)

Shaping the Reading Field (2007)

Poetic Possibilities: Poems to Enhance Literacy Learning (2006)

Collaborative Literacy: Engaging Gifted Strategies for All Learners (2006)

Quotes to Inspire Great Reading Teachers (2006)

Metacognition in Literacy Learning (2005)

Reading First and Beyond (2005)